Copyright © 2012
Marc Bullard
YouTube Guidebook

http://www.MarcBullard.com

YouTube Guidebook

Video Marketing for Businesses, Entrepreneurs, and Internet Stars.

by Marc Bullard

http://www.MarcBullard.com

YouTube Guidebook

Welcome to the YouTube Guidebook. If you're thinking about starting a video marketing campaign or if you already have one that could use some work, this book is for you.

The YouTube Guidebook provides you step-by-step instruction on how to use virtually every feature of YouTube, and more importantly, on how to use it for marketing. No matter how proficient you are with YouTube's many features (or not) I'm sure there is something in this book you never knew. A few of the lessons provided in this book include:

- How important video marketing is now and **will** be in the future
- How to get better search engine positioning with videos
- How to upload and optimize your YouTube videos
- How to optimize and maximize your YouTube channel
- How to search for popular videos and what to do with them
- How to research trending videos
- How to find the next upcoming viral videos
- How to structure your videos
- What equipment you should use (it's cheaper than you think)
- Discover the most popular videos and what to do with them.
- Popular tools to help you discover new demographics
- Helpful tools to enjoy and customize YouTube videos
- Step-by-step instruction
- Much, much, more

Let's not be formal here. This book is written as if I'm training you myself. The sentences will be written as if I'm having a conversation with you. Hey, that's just my style. What can I say? How about, let's get started.

The Importance of Video

Video marketing is one of the fastest growing and most powerful ways to spread information around the Internet. Online video has become easier to use over the years with better quality players and more vivid video formats.

With the ever growing advancements in software and technology, you can get a consumer level camera and inexpensive video editing software to create informative productions to use on websites, advertising and marketing of your business.

If you think about using video as advertising, this is the cheapest and easiest time in all of history that anybody - a small business person, a person who doesn't even have a business yet, a kid with a skateboard on a trampoline or a multimillion dollar Internet Marketer – can all use the same tool, the Internet. You, Joe Blow, and Joe Millionaire - it's almost an even-leveled playing field. Not taking advantage of it is pretty crazy.

The Internet is not television. Remember that. If you think about television 20 years ago, that was really the only place to get commercials seen other than print ads. It was the only place that you could get motion, moving pictures, and your product or services seen. You had to pay a good chunk of change too. You still do.

You have to pay a ton of money to get your little 30-second promotional video, commercial, or whatever you want, on television. Compared to the cost of Internet hosting, paying for TV ad space is not a good idea. Look at the numbers of people who are watching a certain channel on TV compared to the number of people watching videos online.

The numbers of people watching a TV channel at that time and seeing your commercial are not great. They are so small compared to how many views and how many people could watch your video on the Internet. Not to mention, when you are home watching TV, what do you usually do when a commercial comes on? You either mute the TV or get up and go get a snack, go to the bathroom, etc.

http://www.MarcBullard.com

Online viewers are specifically looking for information on whatever your video has to offer. They aren't going to get up in the middle of your video. If they really had to, they'd pause it and come back. You are getting a focused group of viewers looking for your information instead of interrupting a TV show to throw who knows what type of ad in their faces.

Let's take a look at a stat here quickly. In August 2009, Americans watched 10 billion videos on YouTube. In that same month, Americans conducted 9 billion searches on Google. This tells me that people are watching more videos than they are actually searching for text-based keywords. It's just another point to hammer home the fact that people are now turning to YouTube to search for information more than they are typing in to Google to read about certain topics.

Now, how would you like to have your own station where you can show whatever you choose? You can, and you can have it for free. It's called your YouTube channel. If you have a YouTube account - and you should, it's free - you automatically have a YouTube channel. This channel is where only your videos are seen. There are no related videos from other people, there are no ads, there are just your videos and your information. You can even customize it to look exactly the way you want.

Wouldn't it be nice to have viewers going to your channel to watch what you have up there? They would be less inclined to click out to other sites and more inclined to watch more of your stuff. And the more videos of yours they watch, the greater chance they will buy something from you.

Videos Generate Traffic

Get high search engine positioning

One reason why videos generate traffic is they get high search engine positioning. And that is because the search engines are specifically looking for multimedia; it's called a Universal Search. They want to find all the different media that they can to give the searcher the best experience. In addition, they are especially looking for video. If you haven't made any videos yet, think about how many search engine robots have just passed you by because you didn't have a video to offer.

There could be 200 websites on the keywords 'horseback riding', and there could be five videos on horseback riding. Which do you think is going to have a greater chance of showing up on the first page of Google if someone is searching for horseback riding?

Remember, Google likes to give video suggestions. You'd have a much greater chance if you made a video on horseback riding. Out of those five, you have one of those competing videos, compared to 200 text based sites. Whatever you're niche is, make a video because there is a very good chance that there are many more written articles than videos on the same subject.

Get message out more dynamically
Another reason videos generate traffic is because people get excited. Videos are just more dynamic. Imagine a sales letter that says, "Sensational Sales, 50% off! Click here!" In video, you are talking. You're showing your products, you're selling yourself, and people go, "Hell yeah, I want to click on that!" And they do. You get your messages out more dynamically in the sense that you are using images, you're using audio, you can put text on there. So you have these three tools at your service to get the message out compared to just text.

Embed code allows sharing
Video sharing sites make it very easy to pass your video around. The way they do this is with an embed code. The embed code can go on virtually any

other website and your video can be viewed there. Sharing is one of the most powerful ways to get your video seen and spread. Embed codes help with the ease of sharing your video and also with increasing your views. Any time your video is embedded on a site other than Youtube and somebody watches it, Youtube counts that as a view. The more views you have, the better it looks in Youtube's eyes.

Clickable links in descriptions
Putting clickable links in the description box of video sharing sites gives your viewers the opportunity to go directly to the site you want them to go to. Sites like Youtube have specific places where clickable links are allowed. Make sure you put a link to your site in these areas. If you don't, then how are people going to buy your product?

How Can Videos Help You?

Provide testimonials
Everybody knows that testimonials are gold when it comes to selling your product. Well, video testimonials are platinum. Video testimonials work better because we can see the customer. We can see their face, we can see how excited they are for the product. We can see how thankful they are for the product.

Video testimonials add credibility because they are harder to fake. Anybody can write a great sounding testimonial, add a name of the 'customer', and put it up on their site. With a video testimonial, the person on screen helps other viewers relate. And once you can relate with a potential customer, it's a whole lot easier to sell to them.

Show your product in action
A picture is worth 1000 words. Each second of video contains 30 still frames - or pictures - in it. You do the math. Using video to show your product in

http://www.MarcBullard.com

action is one of the smartest things you can do. Video lets you 'show' instead of 'tell'. Actually, video will let you 'show' AND 'tell' compared to just 'telling' with text.

Do you have a new program you designed and want to show people how easy it is to use? Use video. Have a book that is really exciting? Use video to create a book trailer. Do you offer consulting to large or small businesses? Use video to show what your services are. The options are limitless.

Use as sales promotion
Do you have a great deal that everybody needs to know about? Create a video that talks about this. Do you have a sales letter explaining everything possible about your product, and do you have to scroll forever to get to the bottom of it? Use a video and save yourself a lot of space.

Show your company profile
A great way to stay in the public eye even when you don't have any new products to sell is to use video to show your company profile. Your company could consist of just you or a myriad of employees. Either way, creating a short video saying what you are up to, what's coming up in the future, or even how well you did in the past, is another fantastic use of video.

Introduce your staff
If you have customers who will be dealing with staff members of yours, it can be a weird situation to only know them by email or by a voice on the phone. Showing your employees in a video gives your customers a face to match to the voice they've been dealing with. It makes your business have a personality. This can help customers feel 'connected' to your business, which in turn eases their minds when it comes time to purchase your next great product.

Are you ready to get into video marketing? Well, let's start at the site that started it all...

YouTube

YouTube is the world's largest video sharing site; it's owned by Google, and it has surpassed Yahoo! as the second largest search engine. You read that right, a video sharing site is now the second largest search engine behind Google; and Google loves that fact. Why? Because Google and YouTube work hand in hand.

YouTube is more than just a site for sharing videos. It's trying very hard to be a full-fledged social networking site as well. With features such as adding friends, subscribers, comments, bulletins, profiles, viewer voting, and more, it isn't far off from becoming a giant marketing tool. Most people know what YouTube is but most don't know about all of the features given to each user. Covering all the features of YouTube would be a book in itself so I'm going to stick to just some of the most important aspects of increasing your views, building traffic, and ultimately getting you sales.

Getting people to see your video is one of the most critical aspects of video marketing. The larger the number of people watching your video, the greater the chance they'll buy your product or go to your site.

Using videos is a great way to 'funnel' traffic, weeding out the people who were never going to purchase in the first place. YouTube gives you every opportunity to get your video seen, but most people don't know how to properly use these features.

YouTube Home Page
Once you have logged in to YouTube, you will be taken to your home page. The home page contains many different modules that provide information.

YouTube's homepage is laid out in order make it easy to find all of your subscribed channel's videos. (More on subscribers later.) It also helps integrate social sites with your activity on YouTube as well as making suggestions to videos you may like.

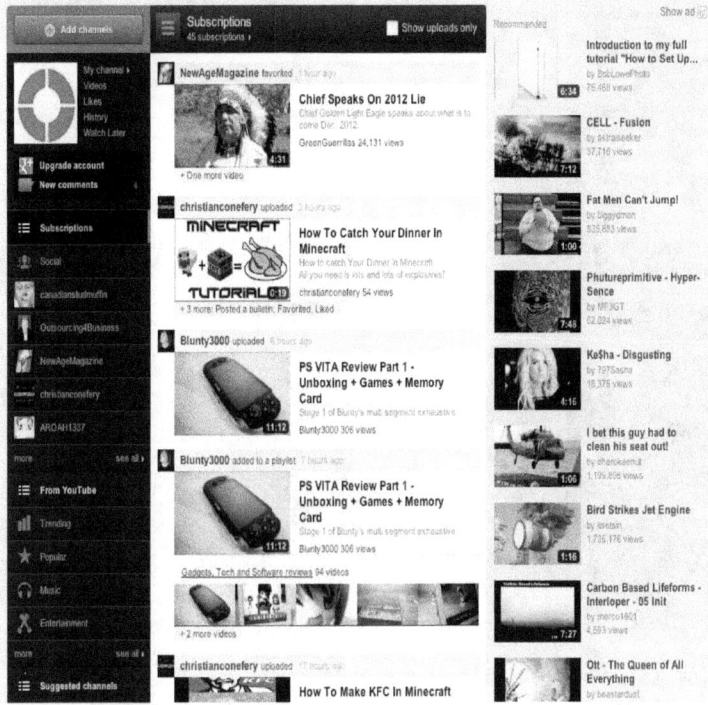

Starting in the upper left, you will see the 'Add channels' button.

Clicking this will bring you to the 'Add Channels' page.

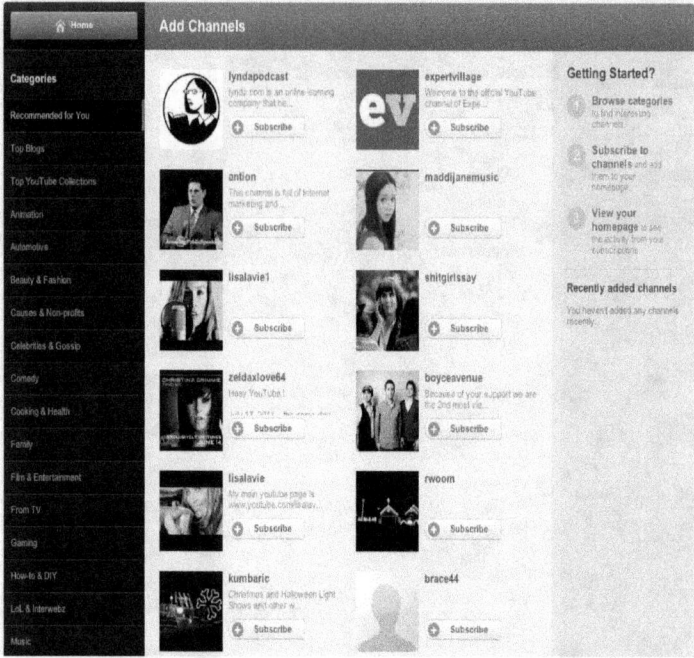

This page provides you with a list of categories on the left hand side, as well as suggestions to channels you may be interested in subscribing to. Looking closer to the left hand side, you can see the different categories to choose from.

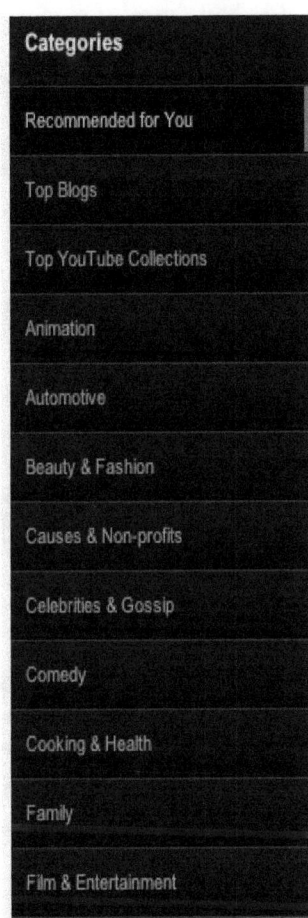

Below the "Add channels" button is your profile information, with links to 'My channel', 'Videos', ' Likes', 'History', and 'Watch Later'.

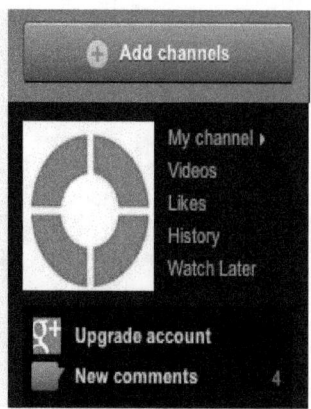

'My channel' will bring you to your own YouTube channel. This is where only your videos will be shown. The goal is to get people to subscribe to your channel.

'Videos' will take you to a list of the videos that you have uploaded. No other videos will be shown. This can help you see all of your videos quickly.

'Likes' will show you a list of the videos that you 'Liked'.

'History' will show you a list of the videos that you have recently watched.

'Watch Later' lets you see videos you wanted to watch, but wanted to watch later. You manually create a list of videos to be put into the 'Watch Later' section.

Below the links will be a place for you to upgrade your accounts with social networking sites as well as read comments that other YouTube users have sent you.

The next section on the left hand sidebar is for your subscriptions. As a YouTube user, you can subscribe to other YouTube channels that are interesting or entertaining to you. This makes it easy to follow these channels, thereby making it easy to view any new videos those channels upload.

The 'Subscriptions' link is highlighted by default when you first log into YouTube. A list of the most recent uploaded videos from your subscriptions will be seen in the feed area of the YouTube page.

The 'Social' link, located below the 'Subscriptions' link let's you see videos from that were shared with you via social networking sites.

Below the 'Social' link will be individual channel links for you to click on. Clicking these will bring you to a page that show those channels' most recent uploads. You will also have the option of looking at more of your subscribed channels or to see all of them.

Below the subscription section is the 'From YouTube' section.

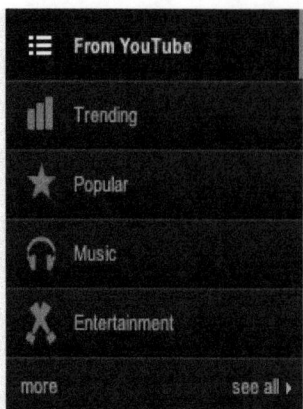

Clicking on the 'From YouTube' link will show you suggested videos that you may be interested in. The 'From YouTube' section is broken down into smaller categories such as: 'Trending', 'Popular', 'Music', 'Entertainment', and more. Clicking on each individual category will provide you with more suggestions related to that category. After looking over the smaller categories, it appears that when you click on the 'From YouTube' link, videos that show up in the feed section are for the most part the top or second video from each smaller category.

Topmost "Trending" video

Topmost "Popular" video

Topmost "Music" video

Second most "Trending" video

Second most "Popular" video

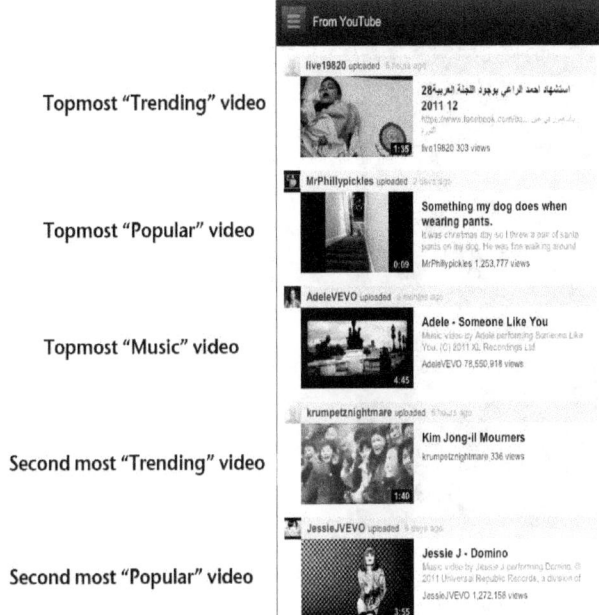

Below the 'From YouTube' section is the 'Suggested Channels' section.

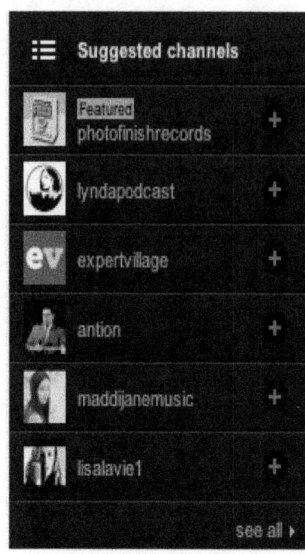

This area shows channels that you may be interested in subscribing to. Clicking on the 'Suggested channels' link will show in the feed the most popular videos from the smaller sub-categories listed below it.

If you hover your mouse over any of the individual channel names, an X will appear, allowing you to remove this channel suggestion.

The right hand sidebar contains Recommended videos. These videos are based on previous videos that you have watched.

Recommended

Wasp vs Tarantula
by RA3DX
145,469 views
3:21

The Four Truths About Boomers and Media
by GoogleBusiness
1,688 views
56:46

Shulman - Invention
by Non3DJ
38,920 views
9:59

Phutureprimitive - Hyper-Sence
by MF3GT
52,024 views
7:48

Carbon Based Lifeforms - Interloper - 05 Init
by marco1601
4,593 views
7:27

accident of a NOAH in mohakhali flyover in
by MrKaushikBiswas
37,440 views
3:32

Zero Cult - Electro wind
by spale13
18,785 views
7:49

http://www.MarcBullard.com

Recommended videos also have the option for you to remove them from the list by simply clicking the X.

Below the recommended videos are Spotlight videos as well as Featured videos. These are chosen by YouTube and can't be edited or removed.

Uploading

Uploading your video is fairly easy. After you have logged in, click the 'Upload' link.

Browse | Movies | Upload

The next page you see is the 'Video File Upload' page. This page gives you the option of either uploading a video or recording one from a web cam. Web cam recordings are great for video responses, they can be made quickly and easily.

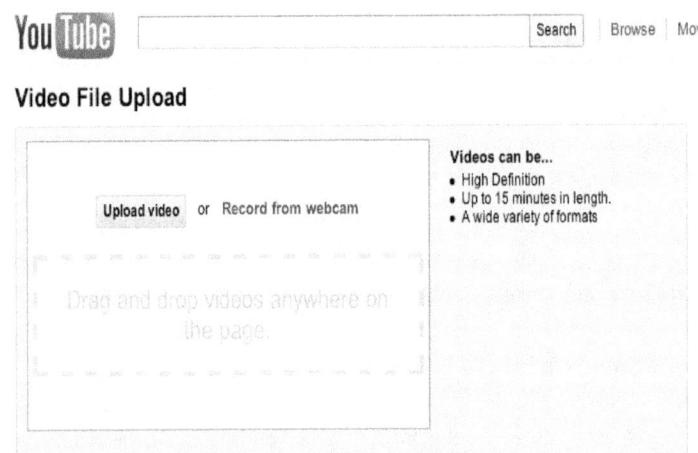

Video File Upload

For our example, we are going to upload a video. Click 'Upload video'. After that, you will be directed to the 'Uploaded Videos' page. This is where you can add details to your uploading video. This page contains 4 tabs at the top: Info and Settings, AudioSwap, Annotations, Captions and Subtitles. There is also an option to view the video on its video page.

The first tab we are going be working in is the Info and Settings tab.

Video Information Page
When you upload a video to YouTube, you have Video Information that you can fill out such as title, description, tags, and categories. In order to get your video seen, you have to make it easy to find. The first box you need to fill out is the title box.

The title box is extremely important. It's one of the first things Youtube and viewers see in Youtube's search results. It also shows up in Google results. Here's the trick to getting people to find your video:

Put keywords in the title
Keywords are words or phrases that the average web surfer would type into a search box in order to get more information on whatever subject they are interested in. Every business has certain keywords related to them, for example: An online health food store would want to get people looking for 'organic', 'vegan', or 'omega-3' as these are words that are being typed into Google by the health food store's potential customer.

Now let's say there were two online health food stores. Store 1 makes a video that talks about all of the benefits of some new vitamins. When it comes time to enter in the title, they put 'Check out these new vitamins'. Store 2 also makes a video about the vitamins but they put in the title box 'Vegan Vitamins - Daily Dose of Omega-3s'.

The second store's video will be seen by a lot more people. Not only that, the people going to see Store 2's video are going to be a more targeted niche, particularly those who are interested in either 'vegan' things, 'omega-3s' or both You can now cater to that niche more exclusively.

I do have a word of warning about the above example. When you title your videos, they must be related to what the video is about. If Store 2 had used that title but the vitamins didn't have any of those benefits, people will click away and you've lost a sale. Nobody likes to be tricked. Be sure to be truthful in your titles.

http://www.MarcBullard.com

Just so you know, be sure to put the most valuable keywords closest to the beginning of the title. For example, if my video was about YouTube Marketing, my title would be a whole lot more important if I title it 'YouTube Marketing – Put Keywords in your title' compared to 'Want to Learn YouTube Marketing?'

How to find keywords
Finding keywords is one of the most important jobs you have to do. Using the right keywords means the difference between nobody finding your video and everybody finding it. Since this is a book on video marketing, I'm not going to go into too much detail but it does need to be discussed.

There are many free keyword tools online, some better than others. There are also pay versions with many more options to choose from. One of the best and free keyword tools out there is Google Adword's own Keyword tool. In order to find it, just type into Google 'Google Keyword Tool'.

Once you go to the site, type in an example of a phrase that your audience might be interested in, for example: Pets.

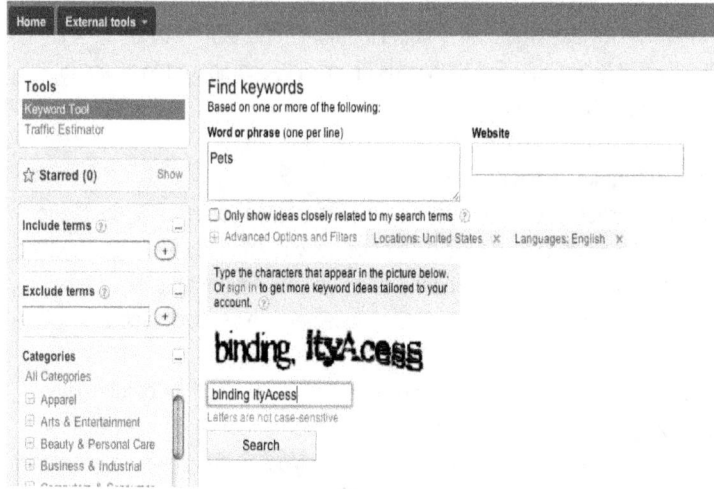

After you type in the phrase in the specific box, you have to enter in a captcha* code underneath it to see the results.

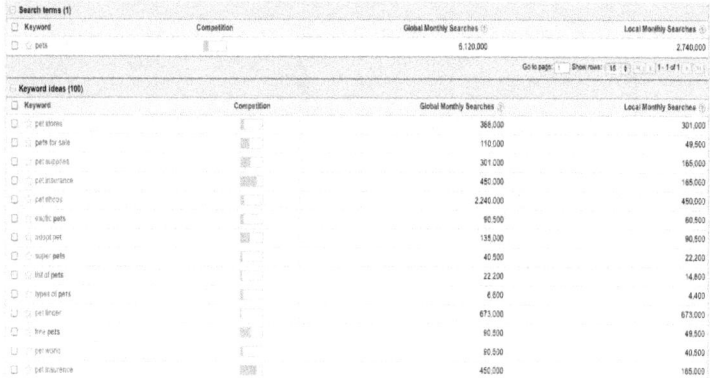

Once the results show up, you will have a list of similar keywords you might want to use in your videos. In order to determine if it's a keyword worth using, take a look at the 'Global Monthly Searches'. The higher the number, the better. You also want to be mindful of the competition. If you place your mouse over the green bar in the competition field, a rollover will pop up telling you if the competition is Low, Medium, or High. The lower the competition the easier it will be for you to show up in search results. Keywords with large Global Monthly Searches as well as low competition are some of the best words to work with.

*Captcha codes are those little forms that ask you to type in some random code to make sure you are human.

Your last captcha submission was correct!

Enter the captcha here. It is CASE sensative!

Submit

You can edit the settings of this captcha in the "image.php" file.

The Google AdWords Keyword tool is a great place to start your keyword research; but it's not the only place.

YouTube Keyword Suggestion Tool -
https://ads.youtube.com/keyword_tool

YouTube now provides you with a keyword suggestion tool all of their own. The Keyword Suggestion Tool searches only within YouTube so your results are different than Google's.

Keyword Tool

Use the Keyword Tool to get new keyword ideas. Select an option below to enter a few descriptive words or phrases, or type in a YouTube video's id (or watch page url).

Important note: We cannot guarantee that these keywords will improve your campaign performance. We reserve the right to disapprove any keywords you add. You are responsible for the keywords you select and for ensuring that your use of the keywords does not violate any applicable laws.

Results are tailored to the languages and countries you choose below:

English		Afghanistan
Chinese (Simplified Han)		Albania
Chinese (Traditional Han)		Algeria
Danish		American Samoa
Dutch		Andorra
Finnish		Angola

How would you like to generate keyword ideas?	Enter one keyword or phrase per line:
⦿ Descriptive words or phrases (e.g. green tea)	
	☐ Don't show ideas for new keywords. I only want to see data about the keywords I entered.
○ YouTube video id or url (e.g. youtube.com/watch?v=JgT4aS5_Zrw)	
○ Demographic BETA (e.g. male or female)	[Get keyword ideas]

Other than choosing a language and country that keywords are tailored to, YouTube's keyword suggestion tool consists of three different ways to generate keywords: Descriptive words or phrases, YouTube video id or url, or by Demographics.

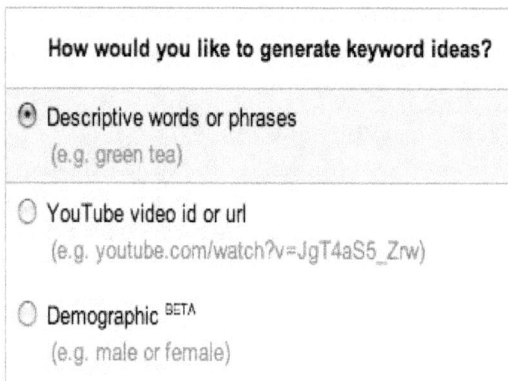

How would you like to generate keyword ideas?

⦿ Descriptive words or phrases
   (e.g. green tea)

○ YouTube video id or url
   (e.g. youtube.com/watch?v=JgT4aS5_Zrw)

○ Demographic BETA
   (e.g. male or female)

The first and default option, 'Descriptive words or phrases' lets you enter in a term and it will show related information.

Type in a keyword term or phrase and click the 'Get keyword ideas' button. **Do not** select 'Don't show ideas for new keywords' unless you only want to see how many people are searching for only that one specific term.

http://www.MarcBullard.com

Depending on what keyword term or phrase you used, your results may differ from the above example. Here you will see other related terms as well as the monthly search volume and an option to add that term to your Adwords account. There may be terms that have 'Not Enough Data' in the monthly search volume as well. This means that there may be searches for these terms but not enough to formulate a number.

That **does not** mean you should ignore these lower value keywords. This means, it may be easier for you to make videos tailored to these words. Looking at the results should provide you with ideas on tags you can use in your videos as well as ideas and topics for upcoming videos that you create. The more lower valued keywords you can place on the first page (or number 1) spot on YouTube's search results pages, the more you look like an expert in that field. This builds a relationship with the viewer, thereby increasing the odds that they'll subscribe to your channel or buy your product.

YouTube video id or url
You can search for keywords that are related to any video on YouTube. Just copy the URL of a YouTube video and paste it into the correct field. Click 'Get keyword ideas' and look at your results.

This is very handy when you want to look at your competition's tags. You can copy these tags and paste them in your videos to better optimize for SEO.

The third option is to search by demographics.

You can search by gender, min age/max age, by country, and by interests.

Searching by interest lets you choose categories or subcategories. Add these to the 'Selected interests' window and then click 'Get keyword ideas'. These keyword ideas can then be used to create targeted videos on those subjects.

A good practice would be to use numerous different keyword tools when researching topics. Never rely on just one keyword tool. There are many more detailed write-ups on finding keywords. This is just a basic summary of how to get started. For more information, be sure to do your research. Anyway, back to uploading.

Description

The next box you encounter is the Description box. The description box is a great place to enter in text on what your video is about. YouTube looks at what you put in the description box, so it's good to put keywords in your description.

Now don't go typing in a list of keywords in your description box, you have to sprinkle them into your description and they have to sound natural. Take a look at a correctly formatted description below.

Description:

http://www.topinternetconsulting.com All you authors out there, start doing this right now. Book trailers are quick, easy to make videos that tell the story of your book. They are just like movie trailers except for your book. You can learn how to make these and how to market them from our Easy Video Creation training series. Also, subscribe to our channel to get the latest from us.

The first thing you see is some HTML code, more specifically, a website URL. We'll get to that in a moment. Take a look at the paragraph after the code. It gives information on the same subject as the video title above. Also, there are keywords such as 'book trailers', 'authors', and 'Easy Video Creation'. This is how you should have every one of your descriptions. But what about that HTML code at the beginning?

The HTML code, that stuff starting with 'http://.....', is the actual website link to wherever you want your viewers to click to. This can be your blog, website, shopping cart, sales page, or anywhere else that you want to send your potential customers. The way I have it typed out is the only way YouTube will allow a click-able link in your description box.

So why do you need to put a link to your site in the description box anyway? People watching your video may like the information you are giving them and are now interested in getting more information/purchasing. Putting a click-able link right there in the description box is the easiest way for them to get to your site. Sure, they could type it out, but I promise you there are people out there that are too lazy to do it. I know I'm like that sometimes. So let's make it easy for them.

Now, why did I put the URL to my site as the first thing in the description box? For a couple of reasons. Let's look at a typical YouTube page:

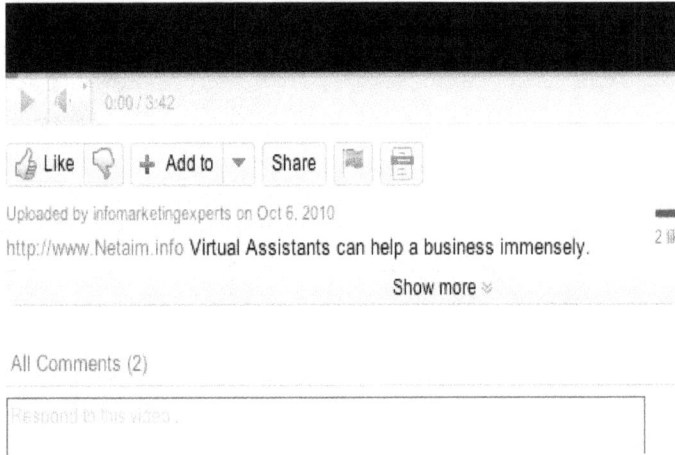

Here we see what a typical viewer gets to when he searches for and clicks on a video. In the photo above, you see the 'play' button for the video and other controls. Under the controls are buttons used for liking, adding, sharing, flagging, and for captions.

Underneath those, you see who it was uploaded by - informarketingexperts - and the date. Underneath that you see the beginning of our description. The description is cut off, there is a button that allows you to 'show more'. If you click on the 'show more' button, the rest of the description can be seen; as you can see in the photo below.

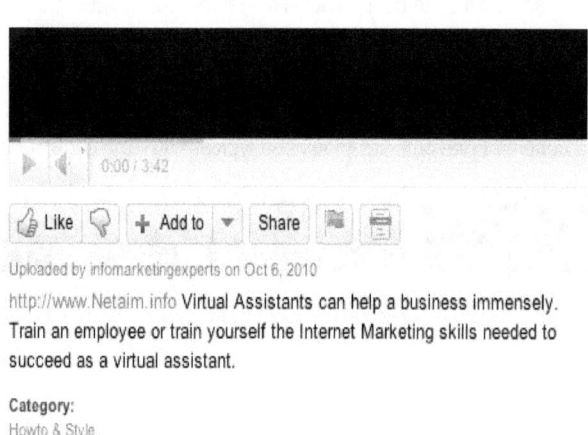

Once the 'show more' button is clicked, viewers can see the rest of the description. The problem for you is that most people don't bother clicking the 'show more' button. That means if you put your one click-able link anywhere but the top of the description box, a lot of people won't see it. That's one reason why you want to put it in the beginning. The other reason to put it there is because it is located right in the line of vision of our viewer. If the viewer needs to pause, play, adjust the volume, or any number of things in the area of the video player, the link to your site is visible.

So why is this link so important? Since the description box is the only place YouTube allows you to put a click-able link, that also means it's the only place anywhere on the page that a viewer can click to your site. It's very valuable.

Tags Box

Tags:

Photoshop email "How to", make smaller files, web ready images, photo tricks, tutorial, smaller .jpg size, photo editing, tips and tricks, software, instructions, help, save for web, fushaka

The 'Tags' box is where you would put relevant keywords. It's important to fill out the 'Tags' box with keyword terms that are related to the video. You can use up to 120 characters in the tags box. A good rule of thumb is to have no more than 6-10 tags in the tags box, so pick the best, most relevant tags you can. In order to provide its users with the best results, YouTube pays a lot of attention to tags, and that's why you should too. If you are having trouble coming up with tags, YouTube provides you with suggestions.

You can also use the keyword tools mentioned earlier in this book. Another great tip when it comes to tags is to order your tags the same as in your title. For example, if your video title is "Business Management: Team Problem Solving Skills", your tags would be listed as: business management team problem solving skills etc. Remember, your tags should mirror your title.

Secret Word Tag Trick

If you've ever watched a YouTube video that wasn't on someone's channel - most people have - you will notice a bunch of related videos on the right hand side of the screen.

Looking closely at these suggestions shows that the suggested videos are from many different users. This means that after a viewer watches your video, they may click one of the others and be on his way. This isn't too good if you're trying to get them to click to your site.

There are two ways to fix this problem. The first way is to direct traffic to your channel (more on this later). In your channel, only videos uploaded by you are available on the right hand side; but not everybody is going to find your video through your channel.

The other option is to use the secret word tag trick, it's very simple and works really well. All you have to do is create a nonsense word, like 'Jamstickerees', 'fleeblinghouse', 'wangchungington' and I could go on and on. It's fun! Anyway, create your own nonsense word and put it in with your other tags.

Do this in every video that you upload and pretty soon, you will dominate the suggested videos. Why? Because YouTube sees your nonsense word and associates it with other instances of your nonsense word, which just happens to be other videos of yours.

Tags are not only important in your videos; they can be a great resource to build traffic too. When you're watching other videos related to your field of interest - and you should - be sure to check out the tags. Other people's tags are a great place to find other terms you haven't thought of and you can find terms that would help your videos show up in other users suggested videos.

Categories

Below the tag box is a drop down to choose your video's category. YouTube pays attention to category as one of its determining factors for finding relevant videos. According to YouTube, some of the most popular categories are 'News and Politics' or 'Comedy'.

If you can somehow work your content into these categories, it could help you out. However, since these categories are the most popular, it also means the competition could be fierce as well. If you can't fit your video into one of these categories, don't worry about it. The other categories are still full of videos and people looking for your information.

Video Thumbnail

The next option you can change is your video thumbnail. Your video thumbnail is the still image of your video that shows up in YouTube and Google search results. The thumbnail has been known to be a huge deciding factor in people picking your video to watch, and yet YouTube doesn't give you much choice in what thumbnail is shown. The video thumbnail box may be collapsed and may look like this:

If it does, click on the black triangle to expand it.

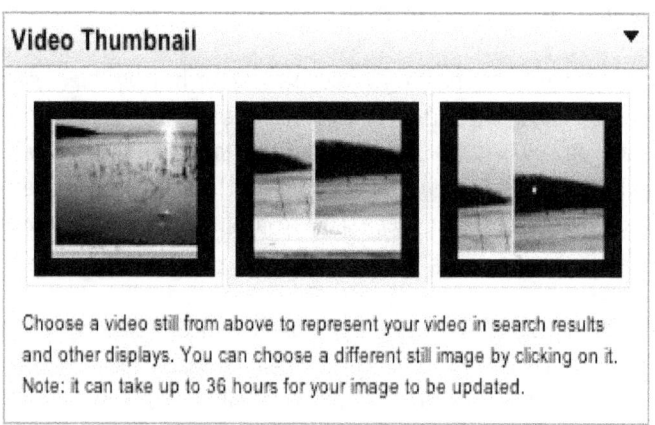

Once expanded, the video thumbnail box shows you three options. YouTube will automatically pick the middle choice for you. You can pick another one if you like. If you have just uploaded your video, the thumbnail stills may not be available to you for up to 36 hours. Usually, the thumbnails will be available within a couple of minutes.

There has been a lot of conversation involved with YouTube thumbnails and how they decide what stills you can choose from. That's right, YouTube decides what stills you can use, not you. If you take a look at your own provided stills, you may be able to figure out the first thumbnail is usually taken from near the beginning of the video. The second still is usually taken from somewhere near the middle and the third taken from near the end.

If you conduct a search about YouTube thumbnails, you might find some people have figured out how YouTube gets these stills. Unfortunately, if you do find such a page, be aware of what year it came out. It's probably from a couple of years ago when you could figure out the algorithm YouTube used for stills.

People realized they could manipulate what stills came up so they would edit into their videos specific pictures at the exact moment that YouTube would make a still. This meant they could 'spam' YouTube and its viewers with a misleading picture used to create clicks. That trick and algorithm don't work anymore. So for now, YouTube is remaining tight-lipped about how they determine stills.

Broadcasting and Sharing Options

The Broadcasting and Sharing Options contains a bunch of different boxes with options on your video. It's important to choose the best settings for optimal search result juice.*

*Search result juice is the amount of good quality optimization a certain video can have. The more juice, the better.

Broadcasting and Sharing Options ▼

Privacy ▼

◉ Public (anyone can search for and view - recommended)

○ Unlisted (anyone with the link can view) Learn more

○ Private (only people you choose can view)

License NEW ▼

◉ Standard YouTube License Learn more

○ Creative Commons Attribution license (reuse allowed) Learn more

Comments ▼

◉ Allow comments automatically

○ Allow friends' comments automatically, all others with approval only

○ Allow all comments with approval only

○ Don't allow comments

Comment Voting ▼

◉ Yes, allow users to vote on comments.

○ Don't allow comment voting

Video Responses ▶

Ratings ▶

Embedding ▶

Syndication ▶

http://ww............................

Privacy

The first box you come up to is the 'Privacy' box. The privacy box provides three choices: *Public, Unlisted*, or *Private*.

Public is the best choice for most of your videos. This option lets your video be found by anybody. If you are using your videos to drive traffic, this will ensure people can find it.

Unlisted means your video is uploaded to your videos but nobody can search and find it. Since you are the one who uploaded it, you are provided all the other options to add keywords, add a description, tags, and so on. The only people who can view an unlisted video are the people who have the URL link. Only you have the URL unless you share it. No search engine will find this type of video.

Private means the video is private and only viewable by people you designate. No search engine will find this type of video.

License

The next box is the License box. You have two choices here: Standard YouTube License or Creative Commons License.

Most of your videos should have the Standard YouTube License. This means you are in control of your video. If you choose the Creative Commons option, your video is free for anybody to do anything they want with it, including editing it. They would, however, have to give you credit as to where that video came from.

Comments

The next box is the Comment box. This box provides you 4 options for how comments will be handled. They are:

• **Allow comments automatically**

• Allow friends' comments automatically, all others with approval only
• Allow all comments with approval only
• Don't allow comments

Now, the best way to get a dialogue going which in turn can make your video very popular, is to select the first option, *allow comments automatically*. The problem with this option is that your comments can get filled with spam. If you keep an eye on the comments, you can moderate any that you think are spam, or you can choose one of the other options.

Allowing friends' comments automatically but approving others is a good way to keep your comments spam free but it creates a secluded feel to the community of your video. Using this option can hurt you when it comes to marketing. People like to see their responses show up instantly; this helps spur along other comments and adds a sense of community.

The next option, *allow all comments with approval only*, isn't much better. It still means that when somebody adds a comment, they have to wait for you to approve or deny it. Most viewers will never come back if they have to wait. The last option, *don't allow comments*, is the worst when it comes to marketing and building any type of social interaction with other viewers. Never select this option if you want your video to do anything positive with your marketing efforts.

Comment Voting

Comment voting means other viewers can rate comments with either a thumbs up or thumbs down.

Viewers who find a comment particularly helpful, funny, smart, or who just agree with what they were going to say can vote 'up' or 'down' on that comment. The more 'up' votes a comment gets, the farther up to the top of the comment page it will go. And being closer to the top is better, meaning it will be seen more often. I will go into comment marketing later.

Awww, I just couldn't believe for song, this just blew my mind!!!!

I freaking love this!!!!

ambient0902 5 months ago 31 👍

Mind blowing.

DubbEighty8 5 months ago 17 👍

The green number next to the thumbs up indicates how many 'up' votes that comment received.

Your 2 options when it comes to comment voting are:

• **Yes, allow users to vote on comments.**
• **Don't allow comment voting**

It's a very good idea to allow comment voting. Again, this adds to the community feel of YouTube. It helps others participate. The more they participate, the better chance you have of them watching more videos or clicking out to your site.

Video Responses

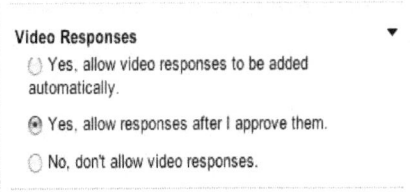

YouTube even lets its viewers leave comments in the form of video responses. This means that viewers can upload or attach a video of theirs as a response to your video. Video responses will be discussed in more detail later. As for right now, you have three choices to choose from:

• **Yes, allow video responses to be added automatically.**
• **Yes, allow responses after I approve them.**
• **No, don't allow video responses.**

The default is left at *Yes, allow responses after I approve them*. This means people can respond but they won't be seen until you approve them. Checking the third option, *No, don't allow video responses*, takes away from the freedom and community feel of YouTube and shouldn't be used unless you are sure you don't want video responses. Choosing the first option is a good idea in order to ensure your viewers have the most options when commenting on your video but again, they could use it to spam. The choice is up to you, I'd recommend going with one of the first two options.

Ratings

After video responses come 'Ratings'. Ratings are used for viewers to vote on how much they like a particular video. The ratings are a lot like comment voting, using a thumbs up or thumbs down to vote. This rating system can be seen located right under the pause button.

YouTube also shows the results of ratings in the green bar here:

11,494

199 likes, 1 dislikes

The 199 likes means 199 people clicked the thumbs up. The 1 dislike means 1
person clicked the thumbs down. We will discuss ratings in more detail later on. As
for right now, you have two options to choose.

Ratings ▼

○ Yes, allow this video to be rated by others.

○ No, don't allow this video to be rated.

Allowing rating adds to the interactivity of YouTube. I recommend you leave it on.
Good ratings can help you become a featured video on YouTube.

Embedding ▼

○ Yes, external sites may embed and play this video.

○ No, external sites may NOT embed and play this
video.

Embedding is the act of taking a snippet of code that YouTube supplies, and
putting that code on your own site or any site that will accept embed codes, which
is a lot. This means if people go to another site and see your video there, they can
play it. If they play your video on a site that isn't YouTube, don't fret. It still counts
as a view on YouTube and all of your video information is still intact. This does not
mean they can copy or edit your video in any way. It does mean that your video
can be seen at a lot of different places, thereby increasing your views. This is a
good thing.

Some people may not feel comfortable having their video all over the web, posted on numerous sites. If that's you, choose the second option:
No, external sites may NOT embed and play this video.
For the most part, you will want this option on *Yes, external sites may embed and play this video.* This is just one more way for you to spread your video all over the web, and that's a good thing.

Syndication

Syndication gives you the choice to make your video available on mobile phones and other devices or not to. I can't see a reason why I wouldn't want this option set to 'Yes...'. If you leave it set to 'Yes...', again, you are broadening your video's scope.

Date and Map
The Date and Map section of your video upload settings is great for relevance and location. Dating a video can help add to its credibility as well as how current the content is. Displaying the date can be a double edged sword. On one hand it will prove how current the content is, however, if you leave that video up for too long, the date can show how un-current your content is. If you keep up with the content and change that video every so often, the date will not cause a problem and probably help you.

Using the map to display where the video was shot can help businesses that focus on local search. For example: a car salesman could make videos showing off the newest deals. With the added information on the map, potential customers know exactly where to go to get to the dealership. Just enter in a name or city in the

'Map Location' box and the marker will move to that destination. You can also drag the marker to your location.

If you are an international business, you don't have to use the map at all. Or you could create location specific videos for your services and post them up on YouTube with the appropriate location on your video's map.

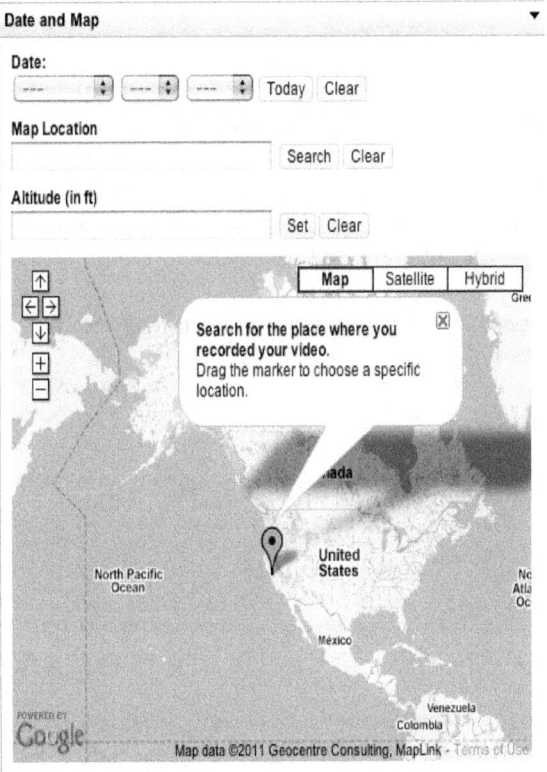

Stereoscopic Video Options

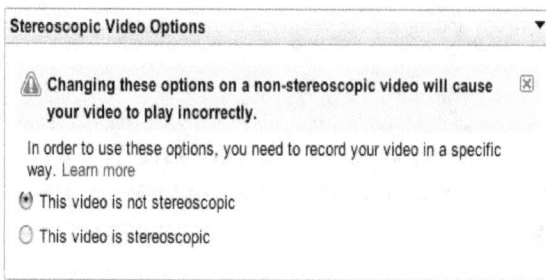

Stereoscopic Video Options is relatively new for YouTube. This option box is for video that utilizes 3D technology. YouTube issues a warning that changing these options will cause your video to play incorrectly. If your video is in 3D, you would want to check 'This video is stereoscopic'. Other than that, leave it at the default setting of 'This video is not stereoscopic'.

Once you have entered in all the options you want for your video, there's only one more thing to do, Save.

Before you leave the page, be sure to click 'Save Changes'. And don't worry, you can always go back in and change any or all of these settings.

Whew. Is that it? Well, no. We still have a few more tabs to take a look at. But don't worry, there won't be a lot of steps involved with the next few tabs. Or will there? (evil laugh)

The next tab we have to deal with is the 'AudioSwap' tab. 'AudioSwap sounds exactly like what it is, it's meant for swapping your video's audio track with another audio track that YouTube provides. YouTube found most of the people uploading videos contained a music track. Often, this music track violated copyright laws that YouTube had to deal with.

Usually, they let you know you're using a copy written track and that the audio will be disabled. This means your video will not have any sound whatsoever, including any narration you have. Most people don't like having a silent video so YouTube came up with AudioSwap. AudioSwap is basically free music for YouTube users to add to their videos.

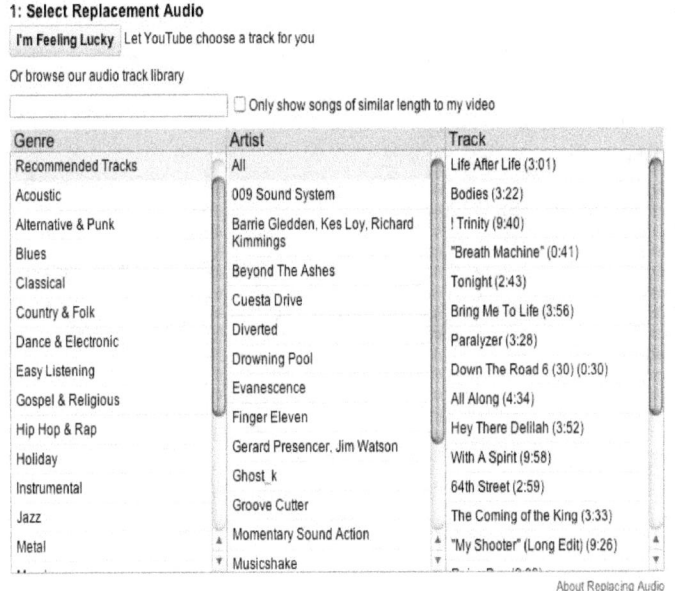

As you can see, there's a pretty big selection of music tracks you can freely use for your videos. All you have to do is upload your video, and then under the AudioSwap tab, pick out a song you want to use with your video.

Track

Astor in Paris (5:14)

B & G's
artist: 3 Leg Torso
album: Astor In Paris
length: 3:40
genre: Country & Folk

If you click on a track, information will be provided for you.

You can browse the audio tracks or narrow down your search to only tracks that run the same length as your video.

Or browse our audio track library

☐ Only show songs of similar length to my video

Once you select a song to use for your audio, you can preview it before it ever gets published.

2: Preview and Publish

Preview with selected track

Once your video is published, it will not have the original audio it had when you uploaded it. Also, if your video has any narration, that will be gone too. AudioSwap is best for videos that don't have any narration, videos such as a slide show type video work best with AudioSwap.

Annotations

Annotations is the next tab available for your video options. Annotations are YouTube's way for you to add interactive commentary to your videos. With annotations you can add background information about your video, create stories with multiple possibilities, link to related YouTube videos or channels, and much more.

If you look at the picture below, examples of annotations are the small link in the upper right, the voice bubble requesting 6 cards, and the text link at the bottom of the screen. YouTube lets you create as many of these as you want. It's up to you to find creative ways to use them.

Interactive card trick

Rate: ★★★★☆

11 ratings

Views: 788

this video has annotations

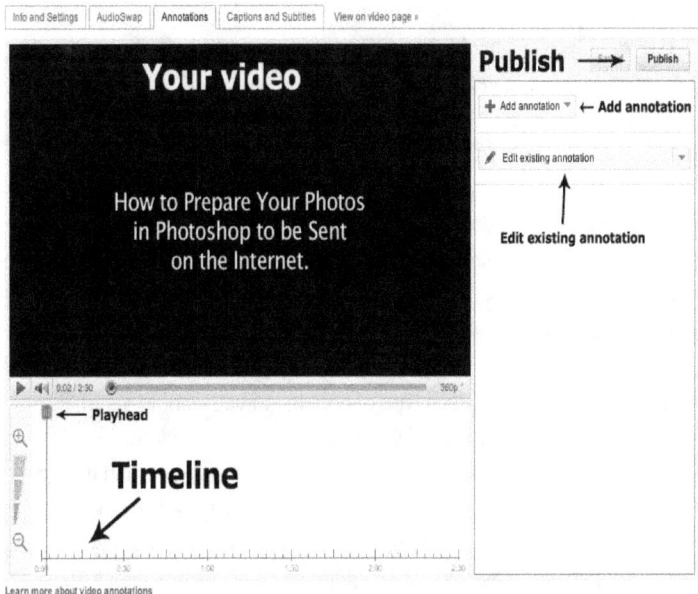

The annotations page contains your video, a timeline, Add annotation button, Edit existing annotation drop down, and publish button.

Adding annotations is pretty straightforward. Drag the play head to the exact location in your video that you'd want to put an annotation. Then click the Add annotation button.

http://www.MarcBullard.com

Choose what type of annotation you want to use. The types of annotations do different things such as:

Speech bubble - for creating pop-up speech bubbles with text.
Note - for creating pop-up boxes containing text.
Title - for creating a text overlay to title your video.
Spotlight - for highlighting areas in a video; when the user moves the mouse over these areas the text you enter will appear.
Pause - for pausing the video for a length of time which you specify.

Once you have selected which type of annotation you want to insert, the following steps will allow you to fully customize the annotation:

1. You can move the annotation that you have created around the video player, customizing its location, or even changing its size and dimensions. To control the position of the annotation with maximum precision, you may select it and adjust it one pixel at a time with your arrow keys, or ten pixels at a time if you hold down 'shift' while pushing the arrow keys.
2. In the Annotations properties panel on the right, you can change the following properties of the text and annotation:
3.

The first option changes font size. The second option changes font color, the third option is fill color. Fill color will change the background color of the box that your text is in.

Below the font and box options you should see options for setting when you want to start seeing the annotation as well as an option to specify when you want to stop seeing the annotation.

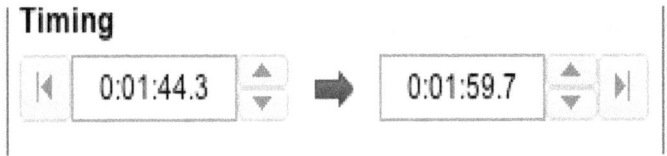

Additionally, you can do the same thing by sliding the blue highlighted section in your timeline.

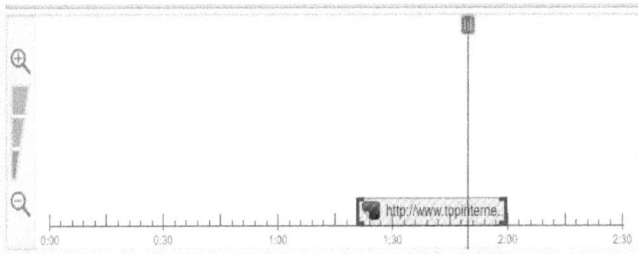

If you grab either one of the darker end sections, you can drag to specific times in your timeline.

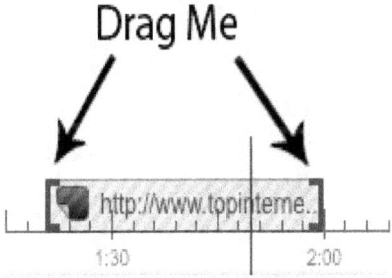

Your video is also available on the same page in order to check your annotation.

http://www.MarcBullard.com

Below the time options is a check box for a link. If you check that box, you then get options to put a link in your annotation.

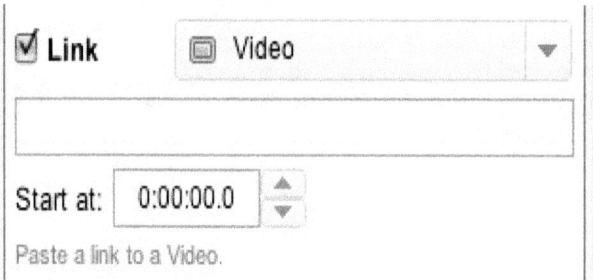

The drop down box provides different types of link options.

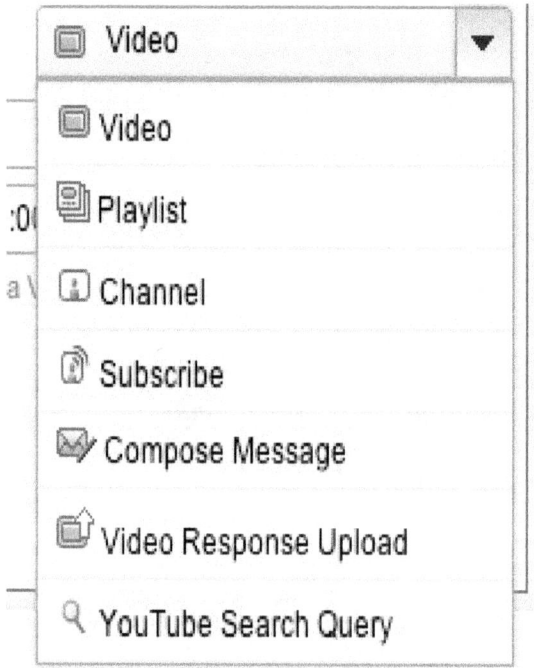

YouTube instructs you on what to do depending on what type of link you choose.

Video Links - Paste a link to a Video. You can copy and paste a link to any video in YouTube.

Playlist - Paste a link to a YouTube play list.

Channel - Paste a link to a YouTube channel.

Subscribe - Enter a YouTube user name to subscribe to. *Usually, this would be your YouTube user name.

Compose Message - Enter the recipient's YouTube user name.

Video Response Upload - You can provide an annotation to your viewers so they can easily add a video response. Your annotation will contain a small square icon that means it's a video response link. This type of link is great for creating conversation about your video. It also helps share your video.

YouTube Search Query - This option makes your annotation into a link that will either take your viewers to certain search terms or to the actual search results page. So, for example, if I chose to put the search term 'Left Handed Babies' in my annotation, when a viewer clicked on it, they would be taken to the YouTube search results for that term.

Search results for **left handed babies**

About 2,320 results

Filter ▼

New Disney Universe Game
Co-Operate Or Compete In An Ever
Expanding Universe. See Trailer Now
by disneyvideogames2 : 73,033 views

Disney **Baby**
Creating Magical Moments
Right From the Start
by DISNEYBABY : 68,431 views

Left handed baby guitarist
Left handed baby guitarist.
by johnnybeane : 3 years ago : 1,820 views

alya aziza muthi, 3 months old, **left handed baby**
adelia jr
by lia2885 : 1 year ago : 38 views

Baby Golfer Hits Backwards and **Left Handed**
17 month old baby hits a golf ball like Tiger Woods.
by jodavincent : 2 months ago : 86 views

See!

"Now wait a minute, where is the option to put my website in an annotation?" Wouldn't it be a wonderful world to live in if YouTube let us create annotations that clicked out of YouTube? Yes, it would. Do they let you do that? No.

Unfortunately, the only thing any annotation can link to is something else in YouTube; be it a channel, subscription, search result, or another YouTube video. Also, annotations can backfire on you. A lot of viewers think they are

http://www.MarcBullard.com

annoying and they simply turn your annotations off with a simple click of a button. So don't go spending enormous amounts of time with annotations, but it doesn't hurt to try a few out.

Annotations are just another way to connect all of your videos with others. And that should be the ultimate goal: Create a networked web between all of your videos, channels, sites, etc.

*Bonus Tip: If you are one of those viewers who doesn't like annotations popping up, you can turn them off either by clicking the red annotations button:

or, if you want to stop clicking the red button every single time you watch another video, go to your user name at the top right section of YouTube and click the drop down box. Then click 'Settings'

'Playback Setup'

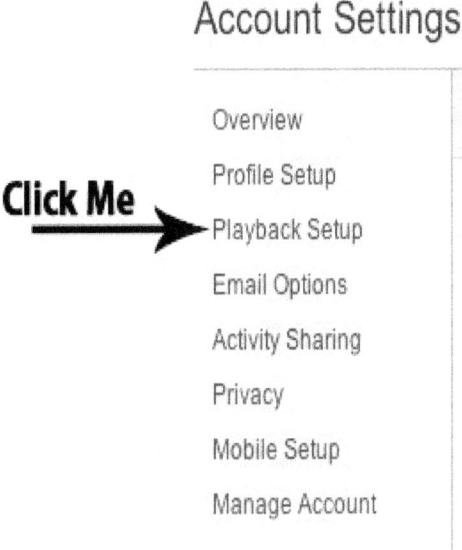

And then just uncheck 'Show Annotations'

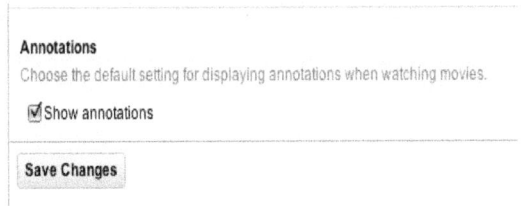

Make sure to Save your changes and that's it, no more annotations.

Captions and Subtitles

The tab after *Annotations* is *Captions and Subtitles*. YouTube likes to make watching video online as easy as possible for everybody. In order to help hearing impaired viewers, YouTube offers up *Captions and Subtitles*.

http://www.MarcBullard.com

YouTube also tries to do a good job of creating a transcription of your video all by itself. If you click 'Download' under the Available Caption Tracks, you can view how good of a job YouTube does trying to figure out what is being said.

Each video is different, but the one I tried this out on had a lot of nonsensical words in the transcription. That's why you want to submit a transcription yourself. In order to do that, click the 'Add New Captions or Transcript' button. Once you do, you'll be taken to this page:

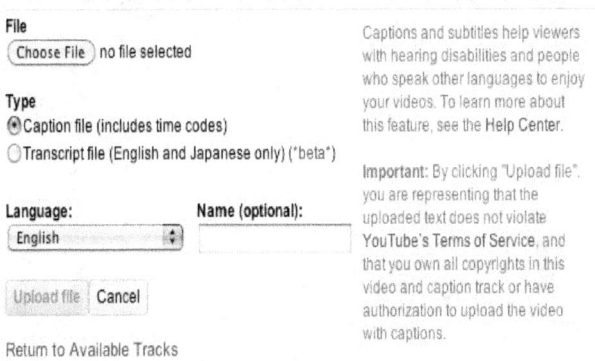

There are two different types of file you can upload. The first one is a *caption file*. This file contains the text and the exact times in the video that the text was said. A caption file is usually made by special captioning companies or possibly the person who created the video. Most people will not have a caption file, which is fine, because the next option, *Transcript File* is perfect for that.

A *transcript file* is going to be a text file of what was said in your video. You can create one of these by either watching the video and writing down everything that was said, or if you have a script, you can use that. Once you upload your text file transcript, your video will now have some new features. Click the *View on video* page link next to the *Captions and Subtitles* tab.

Closed Caption Button

When you view your video again, you should see a new Closed Caption button (CC) next to your annotations button. If you click the 'CC' button, subtitles of your text file will be visible. Another cool feature that your video now has is the 'Interactive Transcript' button.

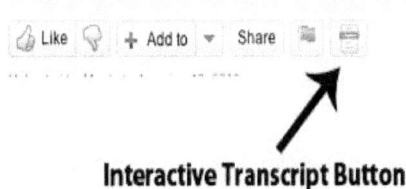

Interactive Transcript Button

If you click the 'Interactive Transcript' button, your transcript will show up.

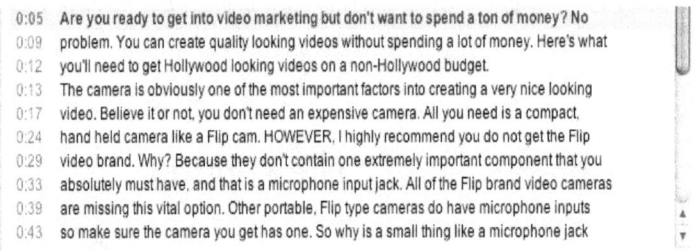

This transcript pops up right above the description box and will scroll through your text as your video plays. Pretty neat, huh? And it's helpful for search results as well.

YouTube (and Google) is doing everything it can to make videos be searchable. Unfortunately, the technology is not quite there yet, but it will be. In the meantime, one of the best ways to make your video have extra search engine juice is to add a transcript. Transcripts are text, and search engines like text.

With an added transcript, you make it a lot easier for search engines to find you. If you click around YouTube and watch some of your competitor's videos, you may see a lot of them are not using the transcript option. Either they don't know about it, or are lazy and don't want to bother. Whatever the reason, it's good news to you. With a transcript, your videos may start to show up higher than theirs, and that's always good.

Views

Now that you know how to upload a video and optimize it for YouTube, it's time to start getting views. Getting views is one of the most important things you need in order to market online. Imagine the number of views as dollar bills, of course you want a high number that continues to rise. The more views, the more chances of getting a customer.

YouTube loves views. YouTube likes to showcase the 'Most Viewed' videos of the day, week, month, year, and all time. Views can also help your video achieve 'Most Popular' as well as other accolades.

There are a lot of techniques to increase your YouTube views and we'll cover many in detail. You don't have to do all of them, but the more you do, the better the result. So let's get started.

Sharing and Social Networking

Sharing your video includes posting it on your social media outlets, on multiple video sharing sites, to your email list, friends, family, etc.

Social Media Sites
Social media sites such as Facebook, Myspace, hi5, Orkut, and more are great places to show your video. These sites work best when you form relationships with other users. Once you have friends on these sites, you can suggest your video to all of them. This suggestion will also be seen by all of their friends as well. They in turn, will watch it and pass it on to their friends hopefully. This cycle can repeat over and over again, thereby increasing your views.

Sharing a video on Facebook

Since Facebook is the largest social media site to date, we'll focus on how to market with your video on there. Most of the other popular social media sites will allow you to link to video in a similar fashion. Here's how to share a video on Facebook:

Before you log in to Facebook, you need to get a small piece of code from your video that's now on YouTube. Go to YouTube and find the video you want to share. There are a lot of different ways to find your video. One of the easiest is to log in to YouTube, click your user name, click the 'Videos' link and find your video. Click on your video's title or thumbnail to play the video. In order to get the code from this page you need to click the 'Share' button.

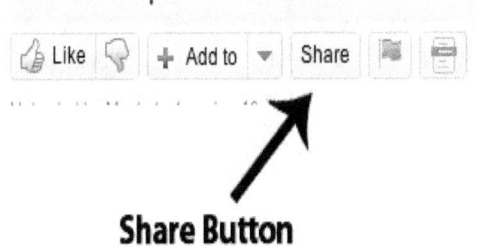

Share Button

When you click the 'Share' button, the box drops down and you see this:

The first thing you see is a box with some highlighted text. Above the box is the text "Link to this video:" You need to copy the highlighted code by either using the keyboard shortcut control/command + C or by right clicking and selecting 'Copy'*.

*On a side note, the code that you copied can also be put in emails, .pdf or word documents, blog comments, forum posts, etc. and it will still be a clickable link. Once clicked on, it will take people to your video on YouTube.

Now that you have the code copied, it's time to log in to Facebook. Logging in requires a free account that you must set up. Once that is set up or if you already have a Facebook account, log in. Now that you're logged in, click your name in the upper left hand corner. This takes you to your wall. You're going to paste the code onto your wall, right in the status box.

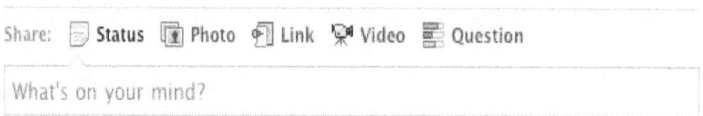

Click in the status box (where is says "What's on your mind?") and paste your code in there either by using the keyboard shortcut control/command + V or by right clicking and selecting 'Paste'.

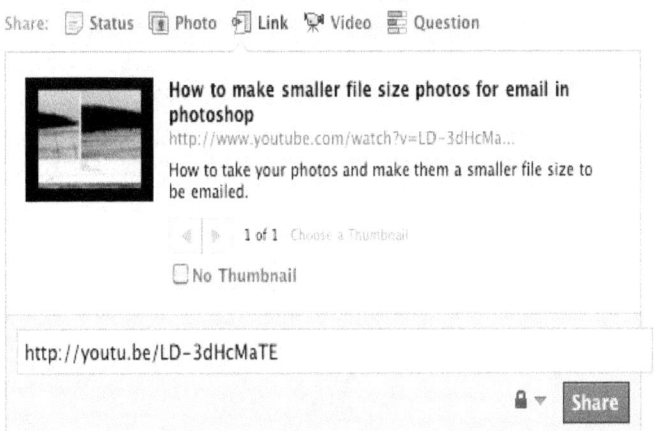

When you paste the code into your status box, Facebook recognizes what the video is. All you have to do is hit the 'Share' button and that's it. All of your friends will now see that you posted a video. Every time somebody clicks 'play' in *Facebook* to watch your video, a view gets added to that video in *YouTube*. Your friends can watch it on Facebook, they never leave the site to go watch your video. This is extremely powerful.

Not only do you make it easy for the lazy people to watch a video by not forcing them to go to another site, but you now have the power of Facebook pushing your views.

Here is a great way to increase your views on Facebook:

Post your video to your wall. After you've posted on it, click the 'Like' link on that post and also leave a comment. The comment should be something to get other people to either respond - "Tell me what you think about this subject" - or to simply pass it on - "Send this to everybody you love".

You want to get conversations going, this forms relationships and builds trust with you. Using the comment to get others to comment or spread your video is a great idea. Your friends have their own friends who you may not know. Those friends also have friends and so on and so on. If your video gets spread and keeps spreading, you will be gaining popularity and views.

When you are in Facebook, you may notice there is a link for 'Video'. So why didn't we use that?

Say What?

We didn't use the 'Video' link because that is used to upload a video directly to your Facebook account. Our goal was to increase YouTube views, so we had to use the YouTube link. The next thing I would do, however, is I would upload the same video to Facebook by clicking on this link. This will give you the option to record a video using your web cam or uploading from your computer.

I would choose to upload from my computer and then I would select the video file from my hard drive, the same video file that I uploaded to YouTube, and then upload that to Facebook. Now, your video will always be available to be seen on your Facebook page as well.*

*Make sure you post your YouTube link on your wall BEFORE you ever upload the same video file directly to Facebook. The YouTube link should be the first time anybody has seen your video. More people will be inclined to see it, thereby increasing views.

http://www.MarcBullard.com

Hey wait, didn't I see the Facebook icon underneath the share code? Yes, you did. Good job, eagle eyes.

Link to this video:

http://youtu.be/LD-3dHcMaTE

Embed   Email this video   +1   show more

Uploaded by Monkstar1 on Jan 10, 2010
How to take your photos and make them a smaller file size to be emailed.
Show more

Hey, wait a minute...

Yes, there is a Facebook button. If you click it, you will be asked to log in to Facebook. After you've logged in, it will share your link on your wall. So basically, it does the same thing. And faster. You got me, I showed you the long way. Why? Why would I waste your valuable time showing you the long way and not this super easy way?

Now that you know where to get your little piece of code, you can spread it out everywhere. Also, just because there's a link to share your video on Facebook, there are a lot of other great places to post your video that don't have a special button down there. For those instances, you'll have to know how to do it my way. So there. :)

Microblog sites
Microblog sites like Twitter, Jaiku, Tumblr, etc. are making it easier to post videos. Twitter has made it easy to show a video while still in the Twitter

interface. Before this change, it was hard to get people to leave Twitter in order to watch a video from YouTube. Twitter's integration with embed codes makes it a great resource to get your video seen. If you don't have a Twitter account, sign up for one. It's free and a great tool to market your business.

Since Twitter is THE man when it comes to ruling the microblogospere, I'll show you how to post a video on there. Posting a video on Twitter is a lot like how you would do it on Facebook. And yes, there's even a simple easy button to post your video for you. Here's how you would do that.

Twitter Link

Find your video that you want to share. Click the 'Share' button. Underneath the code, you'll see the button to share on Twitter (it looks like a bird). Click that button. It will ask you to log into your Twitter account. Once you are logged in, Twitter will come up with the link for you to share.

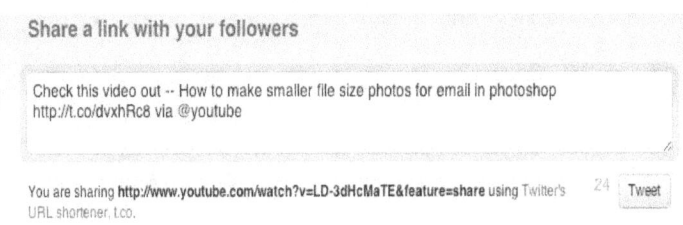

If everything looks good on your end, click 'Tweet'. Your post and video are now on Twitter. Your Twitter post will provide the link to the video as well as a small film icon that, once clicked, expands to play your YouTube video while in Twitter.

Film Icon

Click the film icon to see your video.

http://www.MarcBullard.com

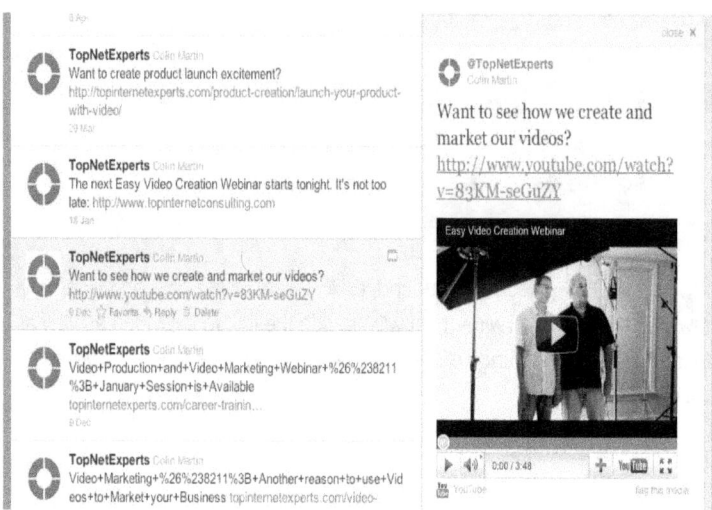

The video plays while inside Twitter. The views however, count towards your YouTube video.

Just so you know, the slower albeit more functional method of copying your YouTube link and pasting it into your Twitter post will get you the same results.

Social Bookmarking Sites

Social Bookmarking Sites like Digg, Reddit, Stumbleupon, and more are great tools to get views of your video. These sites have a lot of similarities with Social Media sites such as having users, a commenting option, profiles, and more.

The difference between media and bookmarking sites is that bookmarking sites are where users submit links to other sites that users may be interested in. Social bookmarking sites break down the suggestions by categories such as keywords, audio files, documents, and video. These sites make it easy to submit your video to a large audience.

http://www.MarcBullard.com

Digg is one of the most popular social bookmarking sites so we'll focus on that one for this example. However, it should be noted that Reddit and Stumbleupon - although less popular - can sometimes result in a larger audience than Digg. It's advisable to have accounts to all 3 of these. They're all free and can be done quickly.

Once you log into Digg, click the 'Submit Link' button located at the top of the page.

After you click on the button, a small window will open, asking for the link.

Paste the link from your YouTube video into this box. Immediately after you paste it in, Digg presents you with this box.

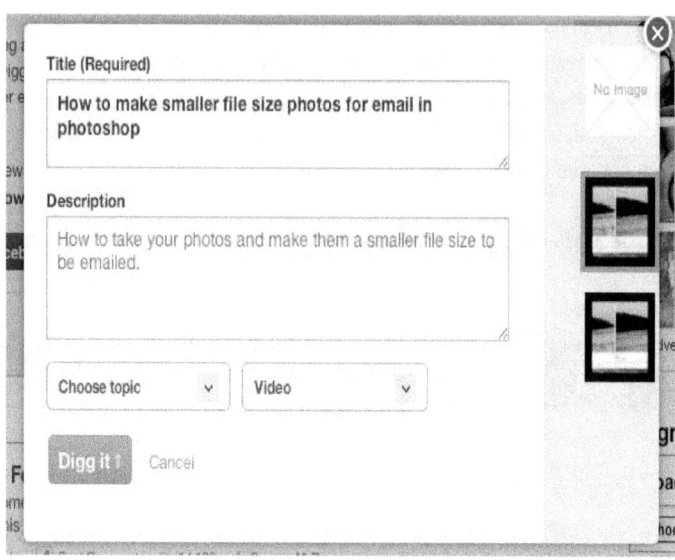

Even though my example doesn't contain any, make sure your description is full of relevant keywords. Also, be sure to pick an appropriate topic.

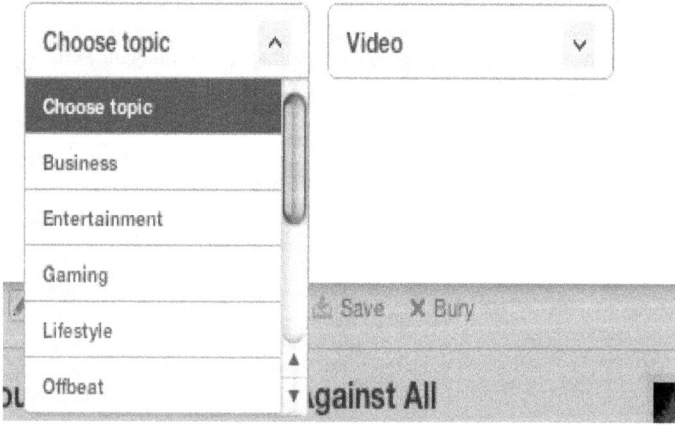

And that's it. See, I told you you would need to know how to do it using the long method.

http://www.MarcBullard.com

Just so you know, the social networking site Stumbleupon.com loves video. It's not as widely popular as Digg but I've noticed in my analytics that Stumbleupon constantly provides results. Be sure to check it out.

Sharing with embed codes

YouTube gives you another option when it comes to sharing your video; embed codes. An embed code is a little piece of code that you can put into your website, blogs, Facebook apps, and a whole lot more. You can access your video's embed code by clicking the share button and then clicking on the 'Embed' button.

When you click on the 'Embed' button, you will be presented with more options.

After making your selection, copy and paste the embed code above. The code changes based on your selection.

The highlighted code (in green) is your actual embed code. If you wanted your video to play in a YouTube player on some other website, all you would have to do is copy this code and then enter it into any place that accepts the code. For example, if I were going to put this video on our Wordpress blog as a post, the first thing I would do is copy the code. Then I would log into my Wordpress site. Once in Wordpress, I would create a new post. In the editor that opens, I click on the HTML tab. This tab accepts code.

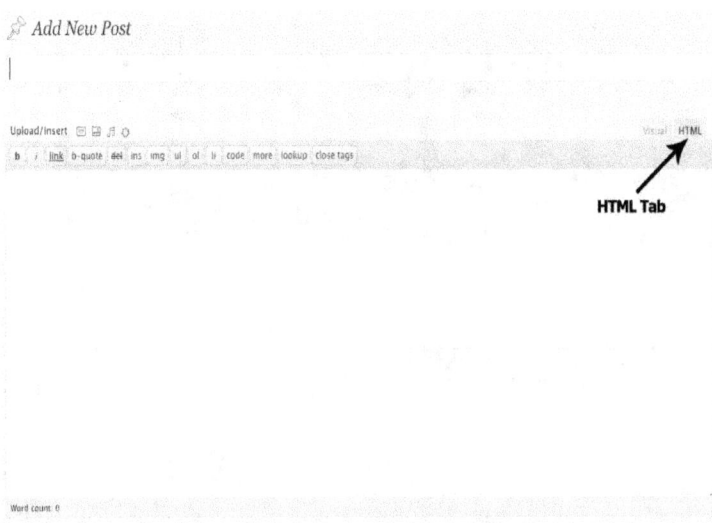

Paste the embed code in this tab.

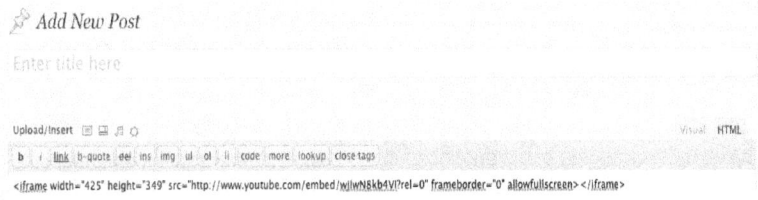

Click the 'Update' button and take a look at your site.

The YouTube video shows up in my blog.

YouTube gives you some options to customize your video within the embed code.

http://www.MarcBullard.com

Show suggested videos when the video finishes - This option is checked by default. This means at the end of your video, other videos will be suggested to the viewer. A lot of people get scared that once their video is finished, the viewer may become interested in the suggested videos and click to watch one of those. This might cause them to leave your site and go to YouTube, never to return again. There goes your sale. If you uncheck this box, you don't have to worry about that ever again.

Use HTTPS - If you have a secure site and want to embed a YouTube video, sometimes an error will come up saying there is 'mixed content'. This is because the embed code is not secure. Check this box in order to avoid the 'mixed content' warning.

Enable privacy-enhanced mode - YouTube has it set up so they generate cookies in order to store data about the user watching a video. In order to give more options over cookies, YouTube provided this option. If this is checked, it restricts YouTube's ability to set cookies. YouTube may still set cookies on the user's computer once the visitor clicks on the video player, but it won't store personally-identifiable cookie information for videos that are embedded using the privacy enhanced mode.

Use old embed code - There are two styles of embed codes. The new version supports Flash and HTML5 video and begins with "<iframe...."

```
<iframe width="425" height="349" src="http://www.youtube.com/embed/wjlwN8kb4VI?rel=0"
frameborder="0" allowfullscreen></iframe>
```

The old code only supports Flash playback and begins with "<object....".

```
<object width="425" height="349"><param name="movie"
value="http://www.youtube.com/v/wjlwN8kb4VI?version=3&amp;hl=en_US&amp;rel=0"></param
><param name="allowFullScreen" value="true"></param><param name="allowscriptaccess"
value="always"></param><embed
src="http://www.youtube.com/v/wjlwN8kb4VI?version=3&amp;hl=en_US&amp;rel=0"
type="application/x-shockwave-flash" width="425" height="349" allowscriptaccess="always"
allowfullscreen="true"></embed></object>
```

Some sites still haven't caught up to the times and won't allow the newer code. If that's the case, use the older code. Other than that, always use the newer code.

Dimensions - You can choose how big or small you want the video to be by picking one of the predetermined sizes or by manually typing in the dimensions in the 'Custom' boxes.

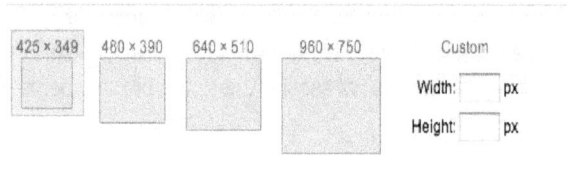

Comments will get views

Comments can be powerful to your videos and on other user's videos. Comments on your video will help get more views, and more love from YouTube. Comments are a big deal to YouTube because they form the backbone to socializing on YouTube. YouTube is always on the lookout for the most commented videos; if you can build comments and start a conversation, it will help you move up to the top of YouTube's search results and be featured on many of YouTube's highlight pages, such as 'Most Discussed'.

So how do you get comments? One great way is by commenting yourself. Your goal is to leave a comment that will either start a conversation, get people to click your YouTube channel, or provide great additional information. Find other videos that are related to your subject or keywords and leave comments that are engaging or that contribute to the information in the video. Any time you leave a comment, your channel name is shown. People can click on your name and go to your channel.

Channel Name

Can I put a click-able link in *comments*? Unfortunately no, you cannot put a click-able link in the comments section, that's why your channel name is so important. Comments are a great way to get a discussion started. Discussions lead to people coming back, which results in more views.

Comments get voted on
That's right, the YouTube community is allowed to vote on comments. Comment voting means other viewers can rate comments with either a thumbs up or thumbs down.

Viewers who find a comment particularly helpful, funny, smart, or which just agrees with what they were going to say can vote 'up' or 'down' on that comment. The more 'up' votes a comment gets, the better the chance it will reach the top of the comment page. And being closer up on the top is better, because it means it will be seen more often.

Awww, I just couldn't believe for song, this just blew my mind!!!!

I freaking love this!!!!

ambient0902 5 months ago 31 👍

Mind blowing.

DubbEighty8 5 months ago 17 👍

The green number next to the thumbs up indicates how many 'up' votes that comment received.

Be sure to leave text comments on your own videos as well as on other user's videos. The next section - Video Responses - will show you how to add a text comment.

Reactions
Along with comments is an option to pick a reaction. The 'Reaction' box is located next to the response window.

Clicking the 'Reaction' dropdown will give you options you can pick that fit your reaction.

Reactions (0)

Your reaction? ▼	
funny	0
incredible	0
classic	0
cute	0
what?	0
ouch	0

You can only add a reaction along with a comment. This feature is relatively new so it will be interesting to see what comes out of it.

Video Responses will get views
Video responses are a form of comment, but in a way they can be more powerful than just a text comment. Video responses allow others to leave a reply via another video. This video can only be from the user's uploaded videos or it can be a video taken from a web cam specifically for that response. Here's how a video response works:

In the comments section, click in the box that contains the text 'Respond to this video...'

Once you click in the box, a newer, larger box will appear.

or Create a video response

500 characters remaining | Cancel or Post

This box is where you would type a text comment up to 500 characters long. Or you can click on the right hand link that says 'Create a video response'.

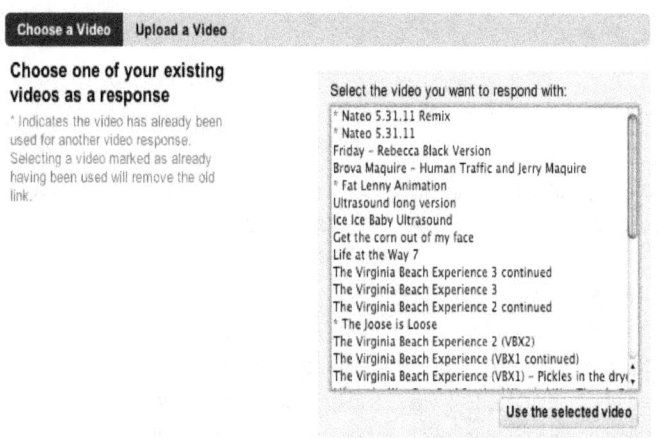

After clicking the *Create a video response* link, you will be taken to a page that lets you choose which video you want to use for your response. The videos provided in the list are all of your videos. Simply select a video and click the *Use the selected video* button. That's it; you just made a video response.

If you didn't want to use one of the videos you already have available, there's another option you can do:

Create and upload a new video specifically to be used as the video response.

If you want to go this route, just click the 'Upload a Video' button next to the 'Choose a Video' button.

If you click 'Upload a Video' it takes you back to the regular video upload page.

Why use video responses?

There are many reasons why you should use video responses.

1. Video responses show a thumbnail - when you respond with a video, your video response shows up as your video thumbnail. This thumbnail image can be used to grab attention of other viewers.

2. Not many people are using them - The number of text comments compared to video responses is measurably different. There may be 300 text comments and not a single video response, which is crazy considering.....

3. Video responses are displayed above the incoming comments - If you look at the comments section, you'll notice the top two comments (decided by voters) and right below that are the video responses.

Top Comments

Pause the video, Press 4

nightlight091 4 months ago 128 👍

It sounds like it hurts for the dude being the board.

SokaRoxMySox 1 month ago 19 👍

Video Responses   see all

Elke (Jacob Singer Mix)
by KorsakowSyndrom
47 views
17:14

Becoming Famous
by F139HEY
45 views
3:29

All Comments (1,919)   see all

Response to this video:

THATS CRAZY MAN! HOW'D U GUYS DO THT!

Dewey5013 15 hours ago

Hahahahahahahahahahahahahahaha.
So sick!

AKut1710 2 days ago

Below the video responses are the rest of the text comments. The text comments change and update every time somebody else posts a comment.

4. Video responses contribute to your views - Posting a video as a response can get you more viewers since you are being seen on other video pages.

If you want to view all of the text comments or video responses, click the 'see all' link on the right side of each box.

Just so you know. Most smart YouTube users will have their account set up so they have to approve video responses before anybody can see them. In order to get other users to approve your video, there are certain techniques that will help. Here's one way to use video responses effectively:
YouTube Channel – New Version

Find YouTube videos that are based on the same keywords as your business. Pick the most popular videos. See if there are any video responses; most of the time there won't be any. Even if there are some, it's okay, post one anyway. In order to increase the chances of your video being approved make sure you do a couple things first:

1. Watch the video you are responding to - It sounds dumb, but be sure to watch the video you are responding to. Why? Because you are going to...

2. Refer to the video in your response - In order to ensure your video gets approved, it helps to provide quality content and to refer to the video you're responding to. In your video, you may say something like:

'I liked your video on list building and I'd like to expand on it, if you joint venture with others in your field it will help build both of your lists. Check out my channel for more information on this subject.'

Notice how I referred to the video I'm responding to as well as adding more quality content. This type of video has a better chance of being approved as compared to simply posting a commercial for your new book as a video response.

YouTube Channels

YouTube channels are your own TV station on the Internet. Channels are extremely important and a lot of people aren't taking advantage of using them. As of press time, you have two choices with your channel. You can use YouTube's old version or the new version. This book includes both versions. Be sure to follow the steps in the correct channel version.

YouTube Channel – New Version

Your YouTube channel is a place for others to connect with you. It showcases the videos you have uploaded as well as provides information about you, your websites, and your activity on YouTube. Your channel also gives others the opportunity to contact you, leave comments, and watch other videos you have uploaded. A nice feature of your channel is the fact that only your videos will be visible. This means there is less of a chance for somebody to click on others' videos, and in turn leaving your channel.

In order to access the back end of your channel, click your user name. A drop down will show you links. Click the "My Channel" link.

This will take you to your channel.

Your channel has the option to have different layouts as well as custom colors or a custom background graphic. You can also show a 'Featured' video, which is showcased in the middle of the channel.

Your channel has three main tabs for visitors, those are: Featured, Feed, and Videos.

The 'Featured' tab is set as the default tab. This shows visitors your featured video as well as information below the featured video. The information that is shown below the featured video is dependant upon what channel layout you choose.

The 'Feed' tab shows visitors what activity has been going on with you (your user name).

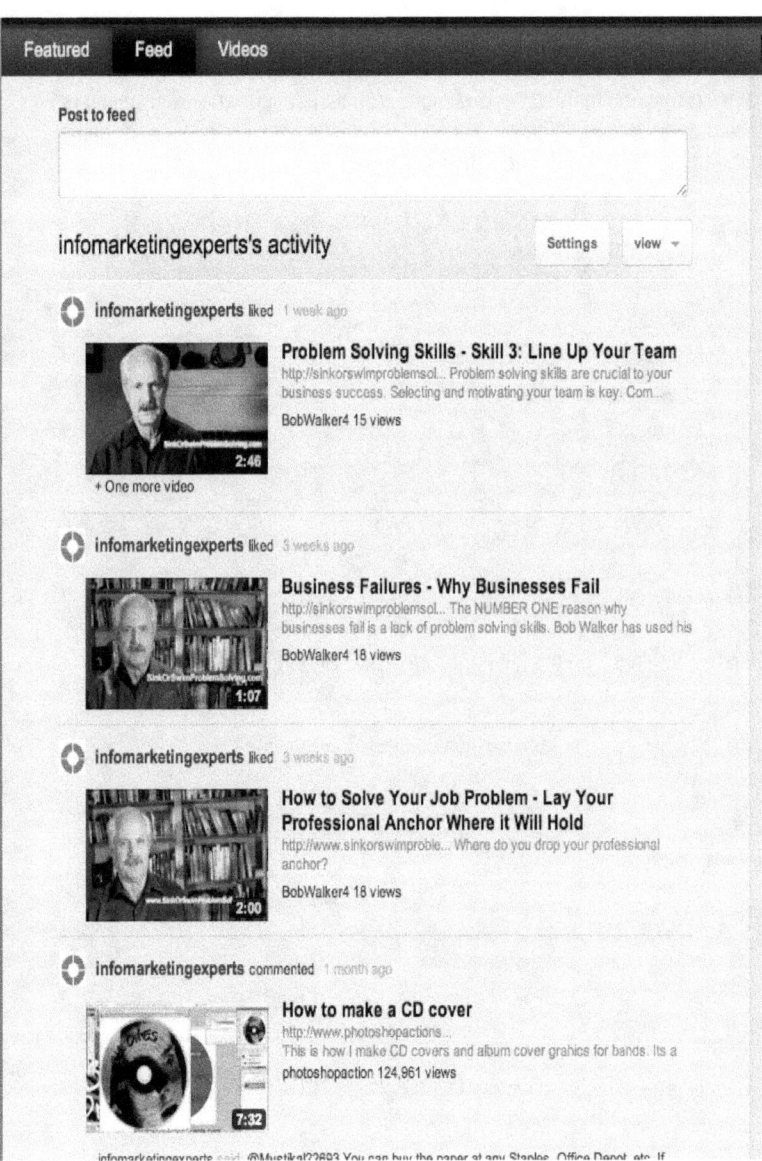

The 'Feed' tab provides information such as what videos you have uploaded, what videos you
have liked or commented on, and more. You can decide what information is shown on your feed. In order to change what is shown, click your user name in the upper right corner and select 'Settings'.

Once in 'Settings', on the left hand side, click 'Sharing'.

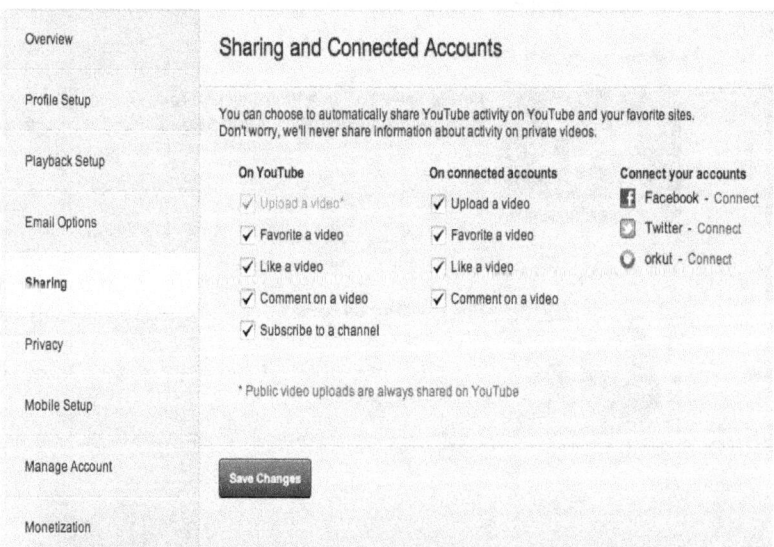

This is where you can decide what is shown on your feed. Uploaded videos are always shown on your feed. You can also decide what is shown on connected accounts as well as connect to any accounts you haven't yet.

Once those settings are determined, go back to your feed on your channel and click 'Settings'.

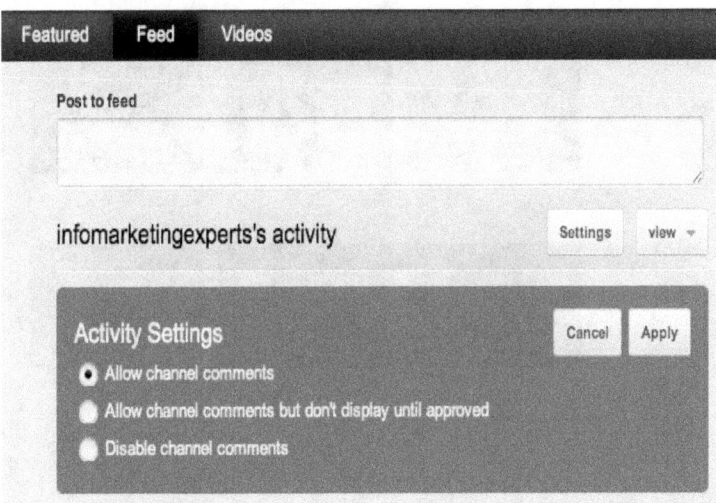

These settings will let you decide on whether you will 'Allow channel comments', 'Allow channel comments but don't display until approved', or 'Disable channel comments'. Most people pick 'Allow channel comments' or wait to approve them. The goal is to create conversations and relationships with viewers. This will get them coming back time and again to your channel. YouTube likes activity like this.

The 'Videos' tab shows visitors what videos you have uploaded. This tab will show playlists you have added as well as giving you the option to sort the videos by 'Most Popular', 'Newest-Oldest', or 'Oldest-Newest'.

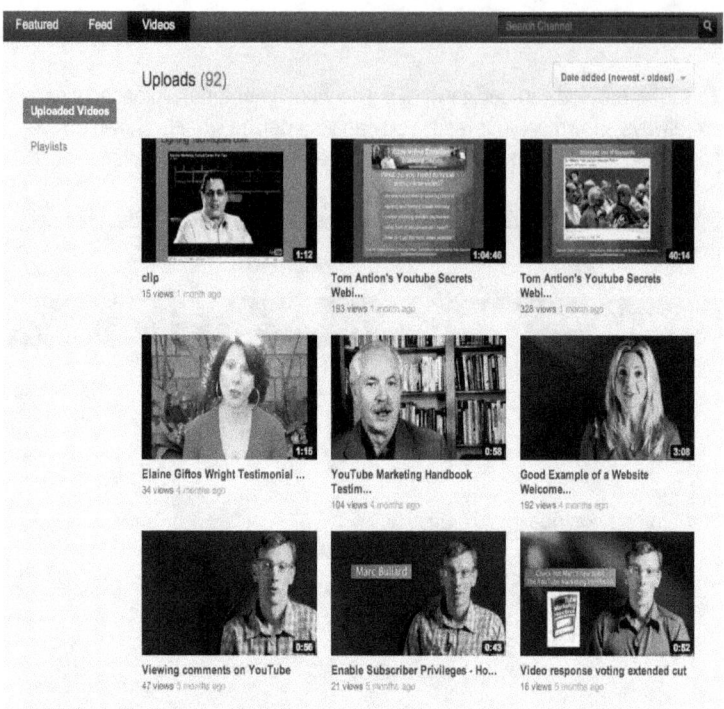

Editing your channel lets you determine how you want it to look and what information you want your visitors to be able to see. In order to edit your channel, make sure you're logged in and click 'Edit channel' in the upper right of your channel page.

Clicking the 'Edit Channel' button will bring you to the 'Edit My Channel' page.

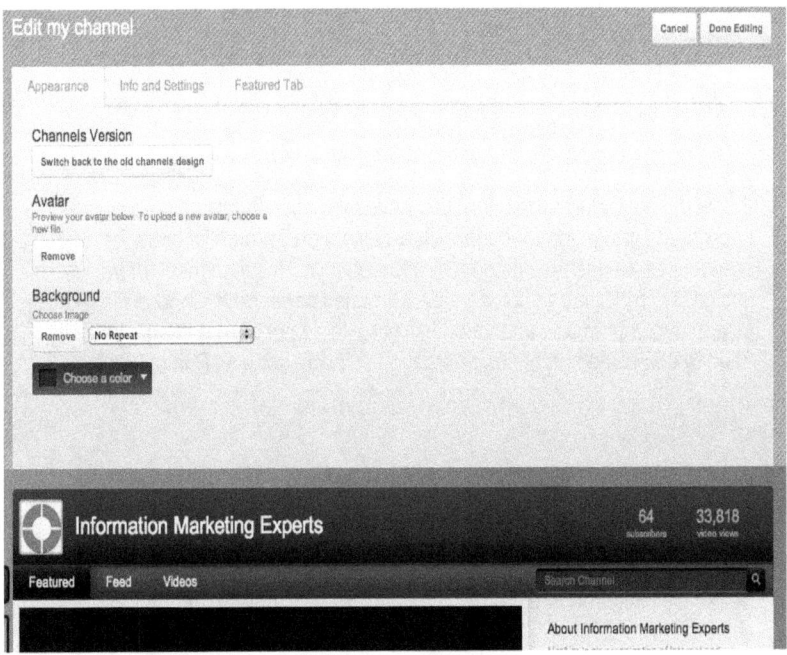

The 'Edit My Channel' page gives you customization choices as well as a preview screen of what those changes will look like. The 'Edit My Channel' page consists of three tabs: Appearance, Info and Settings, and Featured Tab. The first tab is 'Appearance'.

The 'Appearance' tab lets you switch back to the older version of YouTube. It also lets you change or upload an avatar image. An avatar is an image that is used to represent you. It's a good idea to upload an image because this helps with branding and forming relationships with other users.

In order to upload an avatar image you must have it saved on your computer first. Then click the 'Choose file' button. Navigate to your image file on your computer, and upload the image. YouTube takes care of the rest.

http://www.MarcBullard.com

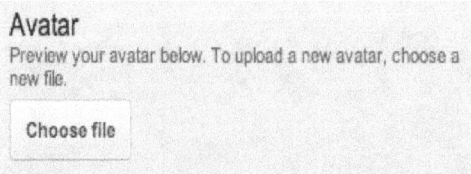

Below the avatar upload button, you have the option to upload a custom background image for your channel. A custom background is great for branding as well as providing more info about you, your channel, or your business. To change or upload a background image, click 'Choose file', navigate to your image and upload. To create a background image, you will need to use some sort of image creation software such as Photoshop.

Below the background button, is the option to select the color of your channel.

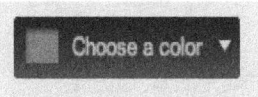

Clicking 'Choose a color' will bring up a color palette for you to pick from.

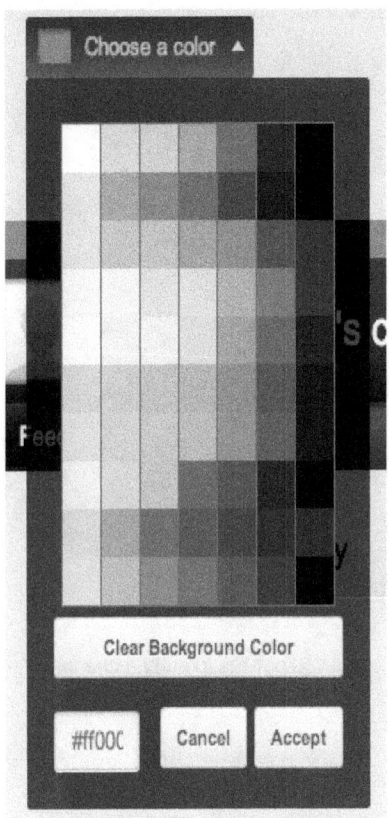

Once you select a color and click the 'Accept' button, you will see your preview screen change to reflect your color choice. Feel free to play around with your color choices, they can always be changed at any point.

The next tab is the 'Info and Settings' tab.

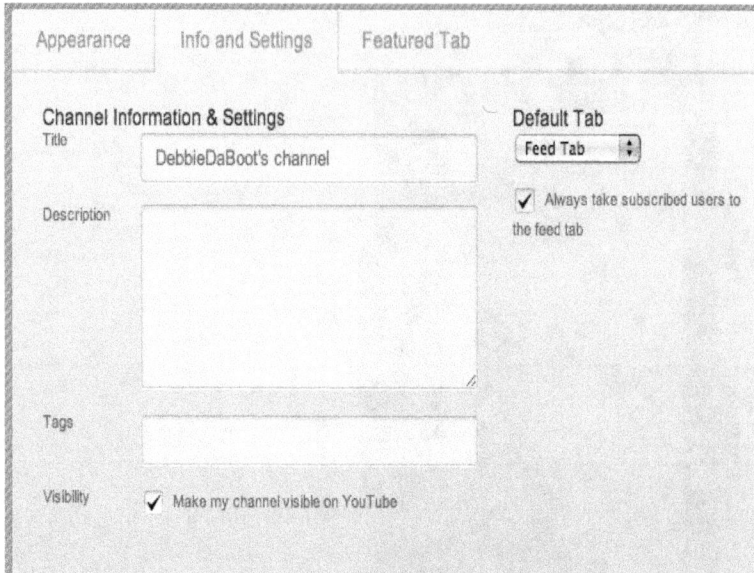

'Channel Information & Settings' page gives you options to enter a channel Title, Description, and Tags. Be sure to fill these out completely, as these will help with search engine optimization.

You can also decide whether you want your channel visible on YouTube by clicking the check box on or off. The default tab option lets you select what tab users see first. Again, your choices for default tab is either Featured, Feed, or Videos. You can also set where you want subscribed users to go to when they visit your channel.

The next tab is the 'Featured Tab'.

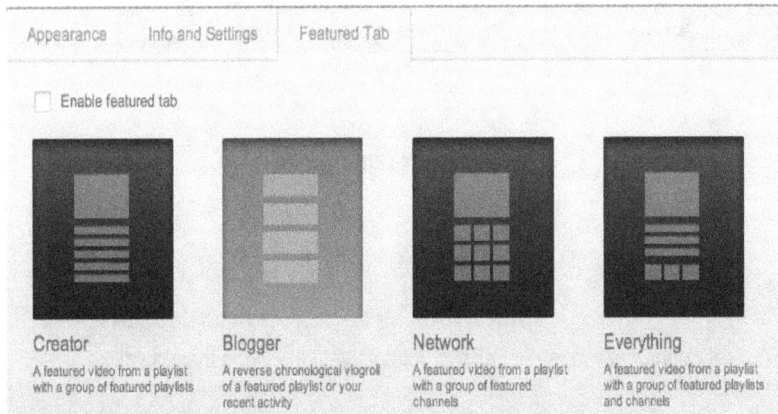

The 'Featured Tab' page lets you pick a layout for your channel as well as setting whether you want to enable the featured tab or not.

You may want to play around with the layout to see which works best for you. However, the 'Blogger' layout seems to be the most popular at this point in time because it lets you feature your uploaded videos, as well as playlists and other channels. That being said, the other layouts have their benefits too. For instance, the 'Network' layout is great for someone who has a lot of channels that they want to feature and 'Creator' is great if you've already got a *ton* of videos divided into playlists. This gives viewers an easy menu to access the largest number of your videos. The choice is up to you, and remember you can change this layout at other times.

If the layout you chose allows you to have a featured video, it's a good idea to put one up.To add a featured video to your channel, just click on 'Add a featured video.'

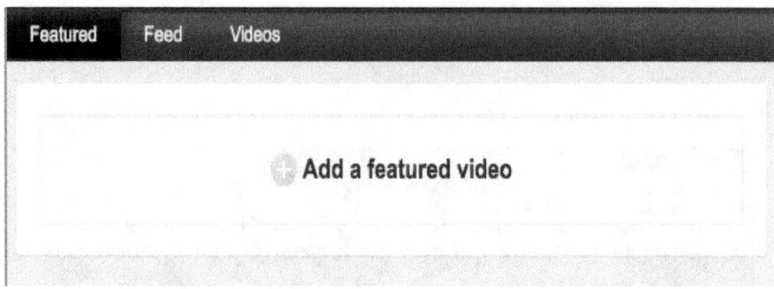

This will open up a widget that allows you to select the video that you'd like to feature.

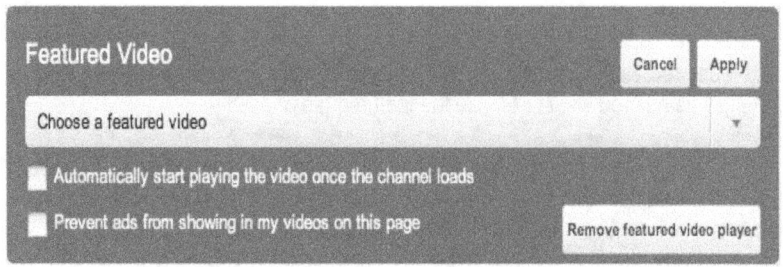

Clicking the 'Choose a feature video' drop down box will let you select a video from your uploaded videos (selected in blue) or one of your 'Favorite' videos.

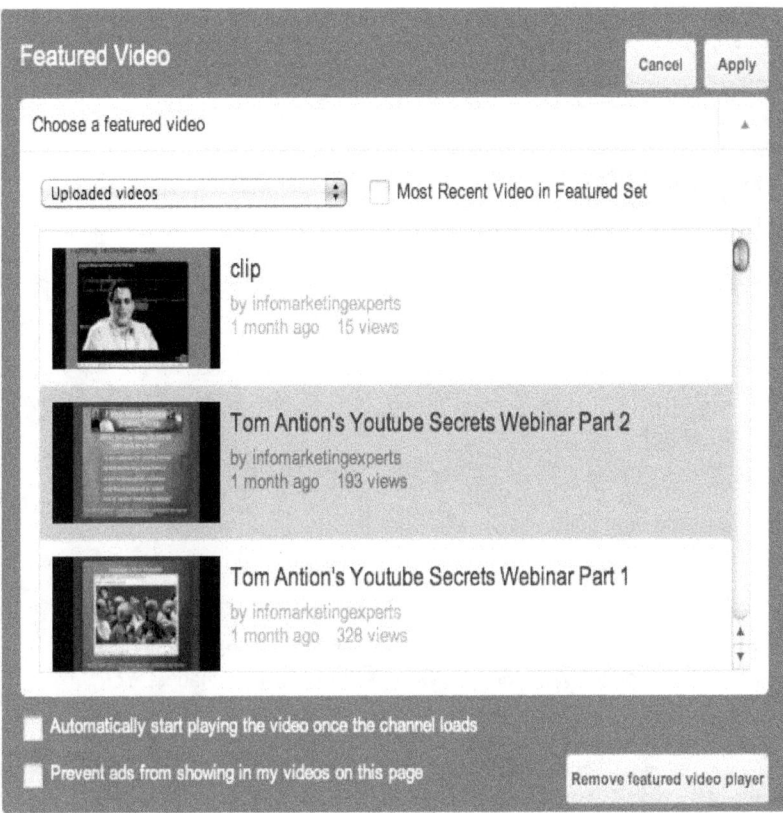

Uploaded videos drop down

Favorite videos drop down

Checking the 'Most Recent Video in Featured Set' box will ensure that the most recently uploaded video will always be featured on your channel. You can check on the box to 'Automatically start playing the video once the channel loads' if you'd like that, but it is not recommended. A good number of viewers find auto-play annoying on a chahnel. If your channel is enabled for advertising, you can also check the box to 'Prevent ads from showing in my videos on this page.' This is your decision, keeping in mind that having ads on your main channel page could take away from the way you showcase your own brand.

- Automatically start playing the video once the channel loads
- Prevent ads from showing in my videos on this page
  Remove featured video player

About your channel section
The 'About your channel' section is one of the most important parts of your YouTube channel page. This is where you can add information about you or your business as well as provide links to other sites of yours. You can also

connect your channel to social media sites such as Facebook, Google+, and Twitter as well as post channel comments using the 'Post a channel comment' box.

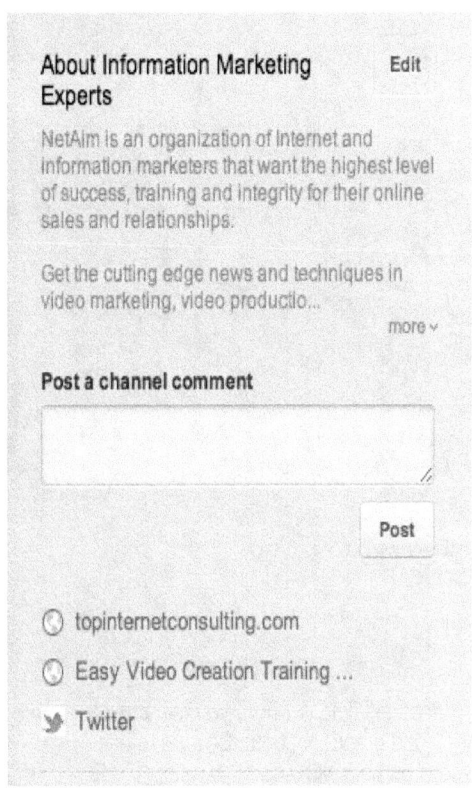

To add and edit information on this section, click the 'Edit' button in the upper right corner.

About Information Marketing Experts

NetAim is an organization of Internet and information marketers that want the highest level of success, training and integrity for their online sales and relationships.

Get the cutting edge news and techniques in video marketing, video production, blogging, reality marketing, social networking, web design, article marketing, product creation, copywriting and more!

NetAim is an information site with two easy tiers of membership. Join big name marketers such as Tom Antion, Jeff Herring, Joan Stewart, Denise Wakeman, Alex Mandossian, Matt Bacak, Yanik Silver and many others!

http://www.netaim.info
http://www.topinternetconsulting.com
http://www.topinternetexperts.com

The first part of the 'About my channel' field is where you can provide a summary of what your channel (and brand) is about. Be sure to use keywords in this section as they can help with search results.

Below the 'About my channel' field is where you can connect with social networking sites.

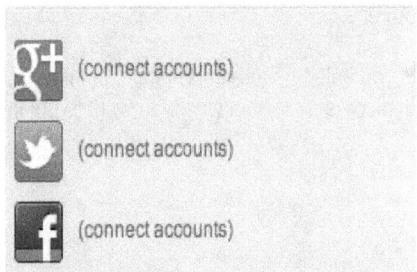

Connecting accounts creates a broader spectrum of your online presence.

The next field is very important. This is where you can add additional links to websites outside of YouTube.

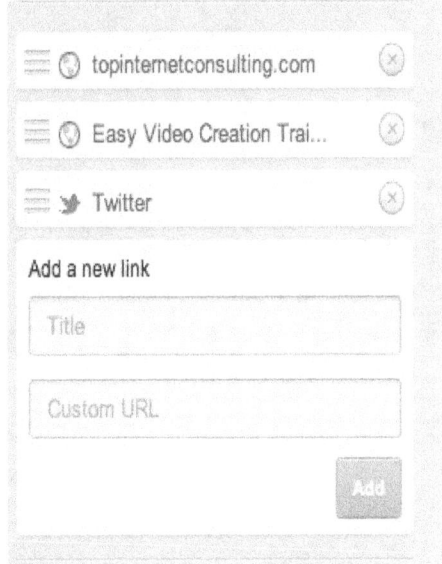

To add links, enter a title for the link in the Title field and add a URL in the Custom URL field. Make sure the URL starts with http://, so a full custom URL will look like http://www.yoursite.com. Then, click 'Add'. To remove a link, click the X to the right of the link. Adding links here is very important. Other than individual videos' description box, this section is the only other place to put a click-able link on YouTube.

The next field, 'About the user' lets you enter in more information, but it's only limited to 200 characters so think carefully about what you want to put in there.

About this user   Hide

We consult in the fields of video
marketing, copywriting, ecommerce,
product creation, and more.

Want more great information on Internet
marketing? Try these:
http://www.topinternetexperts.com

Joined   Hide

Apr 20, 2010

Age   Hide

47

Hometown   Hide

Virginia Beach

Country   Hide

United States

Occupation   Hide

Internet marketing training

Companies   Hide

NetAim.info

Schools   Show

Interests   Show

⊕ **Other Channels**

Below the 'About the user' field, information about the age of the user, when they joined, Hometown, Country, Occupation, Companies, Schools, Interests, and add Other Channnels can be seen in that order.

YouTube Old Version

Custom Backgrounds

You can customize your channel background with a .jpg image. Not only does this brand your company but it also gives you the opportunity to show viewers your face or logo by adding an image. In your .jpg background you can also put in text, providing links to as many websites as you want. This background needs to be created in an image editing program such as Adobe Photoshop or Illustrator. Unfortunately, the text URL's you put in your image background won't be click-able but still, they will be visible. Besides, there are many other places in your channel to add extra, click-able links.

http://www.MarcBullard.com

This YouTube channel has a custom background. The background consists of text that describes what the business does as well as provides URL's to other sites.

Let's say you have a great image you want to use for a background. Here's how you would add it to your channel:

Once you're logged into your YouTube account, click your user name in the upper right corner and click 'Channel'. When your channel appears, there will be some tabs located above your channel; these will not be seen by other users.

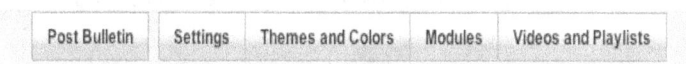

We will cover these later but for now, go to 'Themes and Colors'.

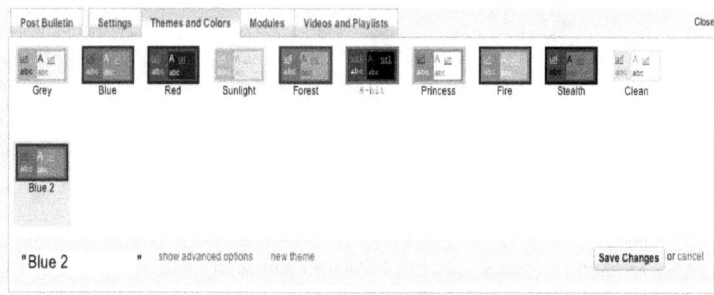

This is where you can pick a color scheme for your YouTube channel. Feel free to play around with these to find which one you like the best. Clicking on any choice will change your background automatically. Once you find a scheme you like, be sure to click the 'Save Changes' button.

But what about the custom background?

Click the 'show advanced options' link.

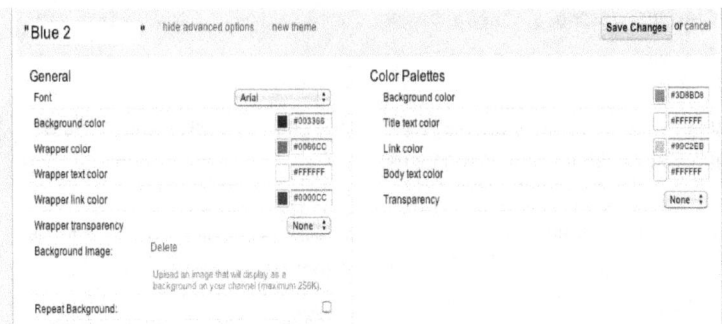

This opens up more options to customize your channel. Here you can change fonts, colors, and transparency. There's also an option for background image.

If you already have a .jpg image, you can click 'Choose File', locate your image, select it, and click the "Save Changes' button. Now you have a new background. If you don't like how your background looks, you can repeat this process over and over until you get it the way you want it to look.

Access to Friends and Subscribers

YouTube makes it easy for others to follow what you are doing with the option of either being a 'Friend', a 'Subscriber', or both. Friends have access to information on what you, the user, are doing. They will know when you 'Favorite' or 'Like' a video and when you leave comments. They will also be able to leave comments on your channel.

http://www.MarcBullard.com

Subscribers to your channel will be notified whenever you upload a new video. Subscribers follow your channel, and not you. They will not be notified of what you 'Favorited' or 'Liked'. Subscribers can also leave messages with you in your channel as well.

Here is how your Subscribers and Friends will show up on your channel:

Of course, you may have more or less subscribers and friends. That's okay, there's always time to get a lot more.

Ability to Post Bulletins and Comments

Bulletins on your channel are similar to status updates in Facebook. This is where you can post messages to your channel. Your subscribers will be notified of your post on their homepages. People can also read your bulletins when they visit your channel.

Bulletin posts are one of the few places on YouTube that you can put a click-able link in, so be sure to use bulletins to your advantage. Here's how to post a bulletin:

Click the 'Post Bulletin' button. Once you click it, you'll see this:

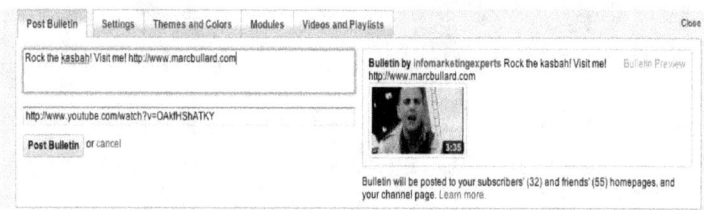

Type a message to your subscribers. If you wish to put in a click-able link in your message, the only way to do it is with the long URL code similar to the one we put in our descriptions; for example: http://www.marcbullard.com

You also have the option of entering a YouTube video URL. Once you have composed your message, click 'Post Bulletin'. Your bulletin will be posted and it will be sent to all of your subscribers. Your message also shows up in the bottom left side of your channel*.

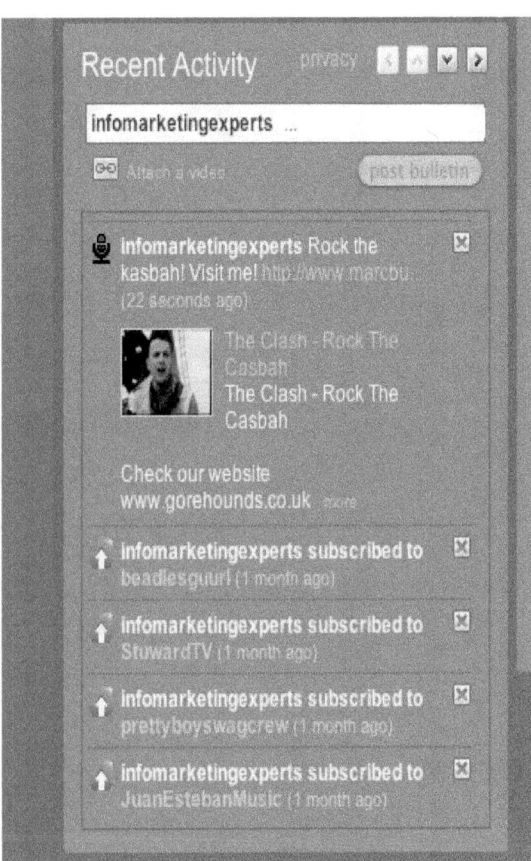

*Your posted bulletins show up on your channel in the 'Recent Activity' module. This module is located in the bottom left of the channel, but that's not always the case. Your channel is customizable.

If you click the arrows associated with the many different modules in your channel, you can move their location.

Click to move modules

Any module that contains these arrows can be rearranged.

Just so you know, you can choose what modules are to be shown in your channel. In order to change what modules are visible, click on the 'Modules' tab in the upper section of your channel and then check or uncheck which modules you want.

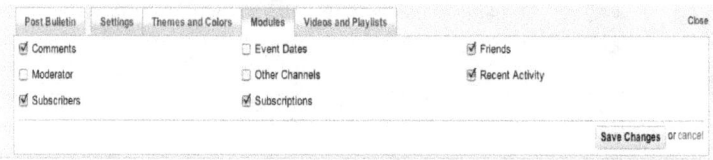

You can also post comments in your channel. These comments are different than video comments in that these are only on your channel.

In order to leave a comment on your own channel, you must post it in the 'Add Comment' box located below your channel comments.

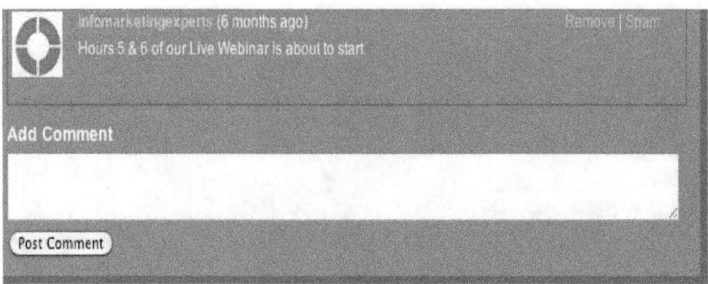

Just so you know, you cannot put a click-able link in your channel comments.

Channel Profile

Having a profile that you can edit is a pretty common thing with most social sites but it is even more important when it comes to your channel. Your profile is one of the only other places to put a click-able link. Not only can you put one link, but you can put multiple links. Your profile is one of the best places to get people to click to your site.

Profile

edit

Name:	Top Internet Consulting
Channel Views:	987
Total Upload Views:	7,007
Style:	Educational
Age:	47
Joined:	Apr 20, 2010
Last Visit Date:	2 weeks ago
Subscribers:	32
Website:	http://www.netaim.info

NetAim is an organization of internet and information marketers that want the highest level of success, training and integrity for their online sales and relationships.

Get the cutting edge news and techniques in video marketing, video production, blogging, reality marketing, social networking, web design, article marketing, product creation, copywriting and more!

NetAim is an information site with two easy tiers of membership. Join big name marketers such as Tom Antion, Jeff Herring, Joan Stewart, Denise Wakeman, Alex Mandossian, Matt Bacak, Yanik Silver and many others!

http://www.netaim.info
http://www.topinternetconsu...
http://www.topinternetexper...

About Me:
Want more great information on Internet marketing? Try these:
http://www.topinternetexper...
http://www.twitter.com/topn...

Hometown:	Virginia Beach
Country:	United States
Occupation:	Internet marketing training
Companies:	NetAim.info

http://www.MarcBullard.com

To edit your profile, click the 'edit' link in the upper right section of your profile.

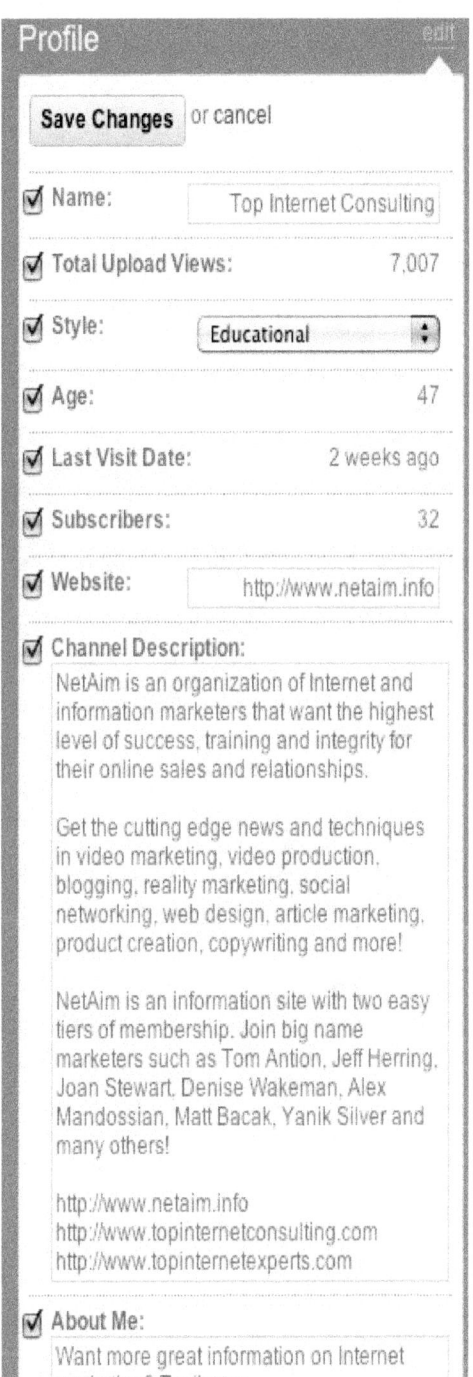

Profile

edit

Save Changes or cancel

☑ Name: Top Internet Consulting

☑ Total Upload Views: 7,007

☑ Style: Educational

☑ Age: 47

☑ Last Visit Date: 2 weeks ago

☑ Subscribers: 32

☑ Website: http://www.netaim.info

☑ Channel Description:

NetAim is an organization of Internet and information marketers that want the highest level of success, training and integrity for their online sales and relationships.

Get the cutting edge news and techniques in video marketing, video production, blogging, reality marketing, social networking, web design, article marketing, product creation, copywriting and more!

NetAim is an information site with two easy tiers of membership. Join big name marketers such as Tom Antion, Jeff Herring, Joan Stewart, Denise Wakeman, Alex Mandossian, Matt Bacak, Yanik Silver and many others!

http://www.netaim.info
http://www.topinternetconsulting.com
http://www.topinternetexperts.com

☑ About Me:

Want more great information on Internet

In your profile, you can add click-able links to the 'Website', 'Channel Description', and 'About Me' sections.

Just so you know, whatever you type into the 'Channel Description' box will be visible in Google search results. For example, we typed in "NetAim is an organization of Internet and information marketers...." and here is how it looks in a Google search result page:

YouTube - infomarketingexperts Channel ... 🔍
NetAim is an organization of Internet and information marketers that want the highest level of success, training and ...
▶ Book Trailers **Marketing** For Authors - 3 min 1 sec
▶ Online Video **Marketing** Techniques ... - 2 min 21 sec
▶ Affiliate **Marketing** - Make it work for you - 4 min 51 sec
youtube.com

So be sure to pay attention to what you write in the description box. It's probably a good place to throw some keywords around as well. (Hint, hint)

Only Your Videos are Available
When somebody searches for a term and finds your video, they will click to watch your video. The video opens in the default YouTube screen. On the default screen, you also have related videos being offered on the side of the screen. These related videos may be other users who are trying to entice your viewers. Usually, once viewers click away, they don't come back. If only there was a way to keep viewers from seeing those related videos...

Channels are different than the default YouTube screen because they don't have any related videos. The only videos available to the viewer are your other videos. This is just one more reason to get people to your channel.

Just as channels don't contain any related video links that aren't yours, they also don't show any suggestions at the end of your video. Here are the suggestions given to us on a video we watched on the default YouTube page:

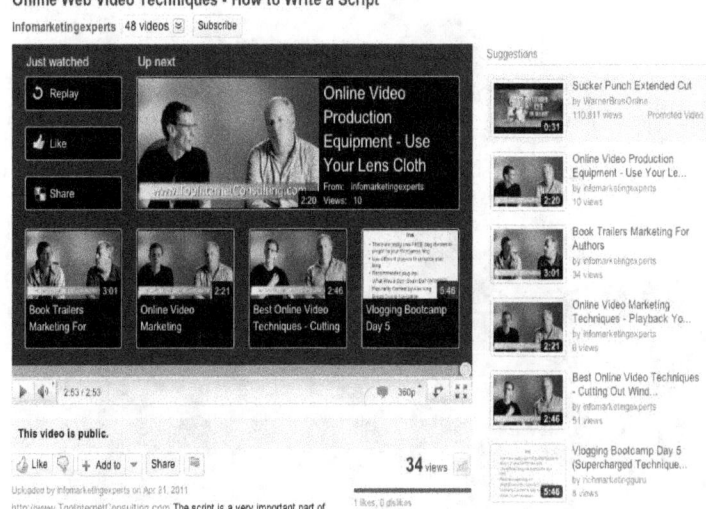

If you look at the suggestions, you'll see the top 4 videos - below the Promoted Video - are by the same user name. That's because we used the secret word tag trick mentioned earlier in this book. And if we hadn't used the secret word tag trick, there would be many video suggestions that aren't by us.

If you look at the fifth suggestion, you'll see it's not by the same user name. Now, if you look at the same video on its channel:

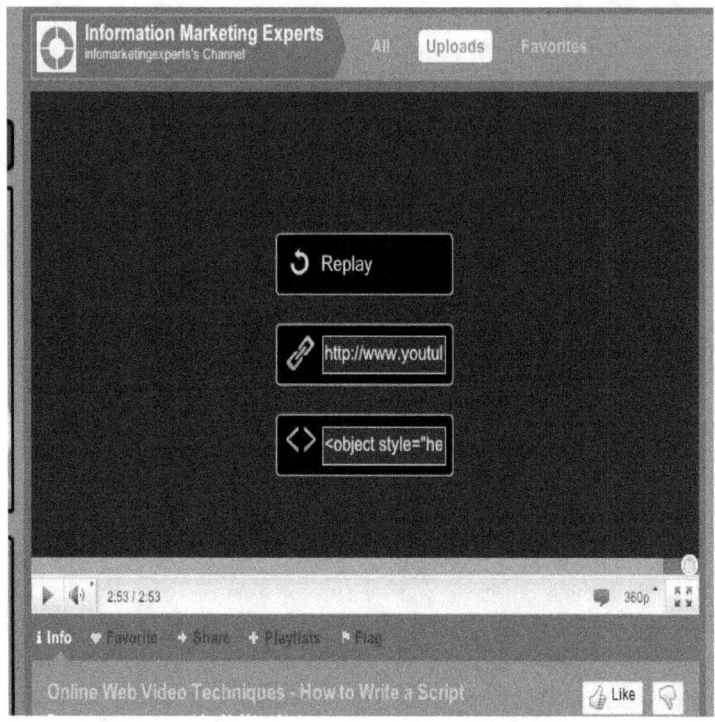

You will see there are no suggestions at all, only a 'Replay', 'URL', and embed buttons. This helps keep people from leaving your channel.

Just so you know, your YouTube channel has its own URL. It's located in your browser wherever you type in web addresses. Also, the easy way to remember it is to add your channel name at the end of YouTube's URL, such as:

YouTube.com/**infomarketingexperts**.

Remember to add the forward slash (/) after '.com'.

If you want to send people to your channel instead of one specific video, use your channel link instead.

Optimizing Your Channel

Once you have uploaded two or more videos, your channel becomes indexed, which means it will now show up in search results. There are a couple of things you can do to optimize your channel too.

When you click on the settings tab, here is what you should see:

URL will display what your channel link is.
Title let's you title your channel. Be sure to use keywords here if you can. Your title shows up in large letters at the top of your channel.

Information Marketing Experts is the channel's title.

Channel Type let's you pick what type of channel it is:

There are different options with each type of channel:

• **YouTuber:** The basic YouTube user setup.

• **Director:** Allows customized "Performer Info" to be displayed on your Profile page, describing yourself, your influences and your style.

• **Musician:** Allows custom logo, genre and tour date information and CD purchase links on your Profile page.

• **Comedian:** Allows custom logo, style and show-date information and CD purchase links on your Profile page.

• **Guru:** Allows custom logo, genre and links on your Profile page.

• **Reporter:** Allows you to describe your Beat, your Influences and your Favorite News Sources.

Other than that, there aren't too many differences between the types of channels.

http://www.MarcBullard.com

Make Channel Visible let's you decide if people can find your channel. If you choose the 'no' button, when people click to go to your channel it will tell them it's not available. If you want to get the most marketing bang for your buck, leave it on 'Yes'.

Channel Tags are just like tags for individual videos.You want to put keywords in your channel tags that are relevant to your videos. You are only allowed 100 characters in the channel tags box, so be sure to pick the very best keywords you can.

Be sure to leave the 'Let others find my channel on YouTube if they have my email address' box checked. This will help people find your channel as well.

After you've configured your channel settings, click the 'Save Changes' button.

Videos and Playlists

The last tab I have not talked about yet is the 'Videos and Playlists' tab. This tab allows you to choose what content you want displayed and how.

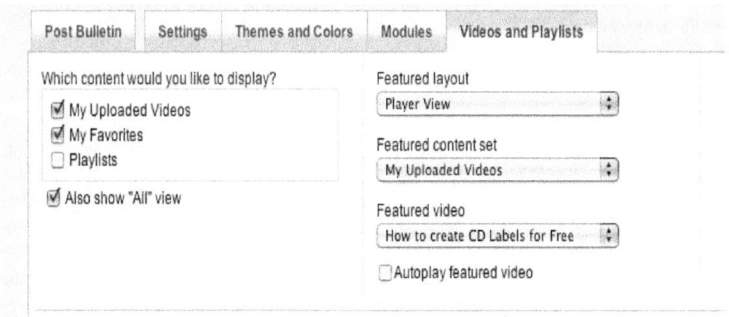

Under the 'Videos and Playlists' tab, the first box you see is the 'Which content would you like to display' box. Here you can choose to show:

My Uploaded Videos - Shows only the videos that you uploaded on the right hand side of your channel.

My Favorites – Shows only videos that you added to your favorites. These videos can be either your videos or other users' videos; or both. Be careful if you choose the 'My Favorites' box. If you mark another users' videos as a favorite, this will be displayed on the right hand side of your channel. This poses the possibility of somebody clicking that video and being whisked away from your channel.

Playlists - Playlists are collections of your videos that play back to back. You can create playlists and then choose to make them visible on your channel. Playlists are great for videos that run in series. For example, if I had two videos called 'YouTube Marketing Part I' and 'YouTube Marketing Part II', I could put them in their own playlist. When somebody clicked on my playlist, it would play part I and then jump to part II once part I was finished.

There are many different techniques you can use with playlists to keep viewers engaged. Having a playlist that automatically jumps to the next video also helps build views. Once that video jumps to the next one, it counts as a view on that next video.

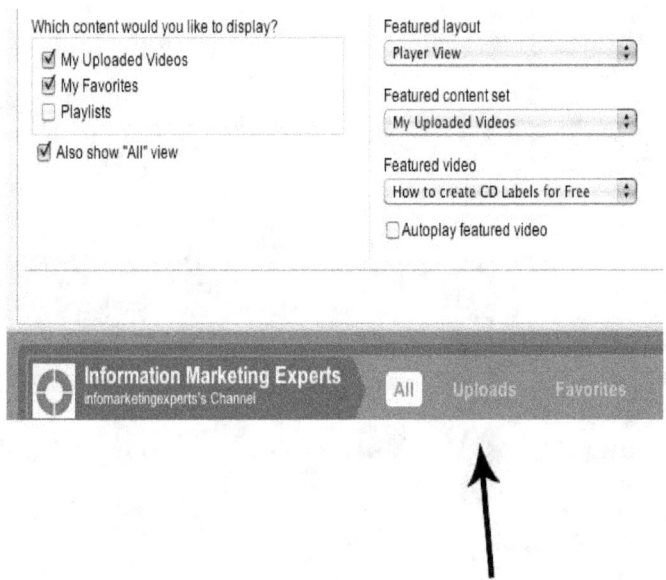

'All', 'Uploads', and 'Favorites'

Depending on what check boxes you clicked, your channel may or may not contain links for 'All', 'Uploads', 'Playlists', and 'Favorites'.

The next option is the Featured layout. In this drop down you have two choices: Player view or Grid view. Player view will show your channel with a main video in the player and - depending on what check boxes you choose - your upload, favorites, and playlists as well. Grid view shows all of your videos laid out in a grid, like this:

Grid view

Most people like to stay with the player view, especially because that view contains a featured video.

Just so you know, your viewers can switch between grid and player view once they visit your channel. So, whatever you pick, your viewers can have whatever they like by click on the 'Player view' or 'Grid view' icons.

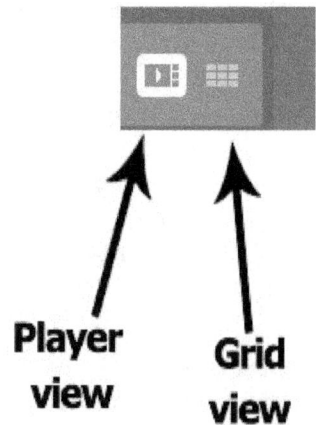

Player view   **Grid view**

Below the 'Featured layout' is the 'Featured content set'. This is used to determine what should be highlighted when somebody visits your channel. If I chose to feature my favorites, I would pick that in the drop down and the next time somebody visits the site, it will look like this:

Notice how the 'Favorite' link in the middle of the page is highlighted and the only video available on the right is my one favorite. The user can still click the 'Uploads' link to see all of the other videos available.

Featured video - The featured video is the main video shown in the large player when you visit your channel. In order to change this video to whatever

http://www.MarcBullard.com

one you want, click the drop down and choose your featured video. You can even decide if you want that video to begin playing automatically when somebody visits by checking the 'Autoplay featured video' box.

A word of caution, autoplaying a video can be annoying if your viewer came to your channel to watch a video other than the featured one. However, if you turn autoplay on, whenever somebody visits your channel it's going to count as another view on the featured video because it starts playing immediately. This is a good way to get some extra view counts. Play around with both settings to determine the way you like it best.

Arrange Your Top Suggested Videos
You can also arrange the top 6 suggested videos on your site. In order to do that, you must click on 'Arrange Uploads' on the right side of your main module.

Once there, you will have the option of picking any of your videos and having them always be the top six shown when somebody visits your channel. All you do is go to the thumbnails of your videos, click and drag the video up to the blank areas numbered 1-6. Click the 'Save Changes' button and you're done. Just so you know, there's also an option to pick your top 12 videos as well.

There are many different ways to use the 'Arrange Uploads' option. Perhaps you want to show the top 6 videos that have the most views, maybe it's near a certain holiday and you'd like to showcase the videos you just made pertaining to that.

You could focus on specific keywords and choose the top 6 related to them, you could create a choose-your-own-adventure with all of the parts easy to get to as the top 6 shown, etc. Play around with those options, any of the examples above can easily get your subscribers excited about your videos again, causing them to re-visit your channel over and over again.

Custom Logo

"Hey, how do you get that cool logo in your channel name and profile?"

That cool logo is your profile picture. If you have a logo, this is another way to help brand you and your channel. You would think you'd be able to edit the profile picture when editing your channel but no such luck. It's actually located in your account settings.

Click your user name in the upper right of the page and go to 'Settings'.

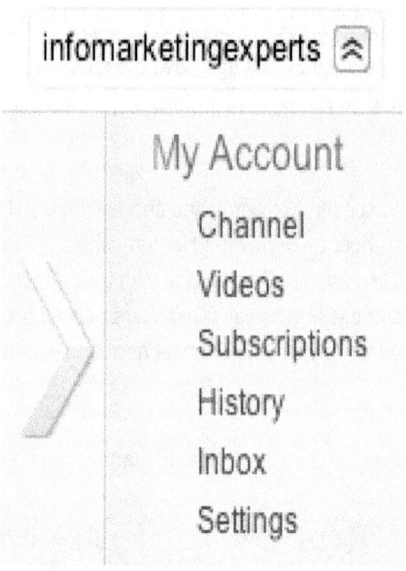

Once you are in your account settings, click 'Overview'.

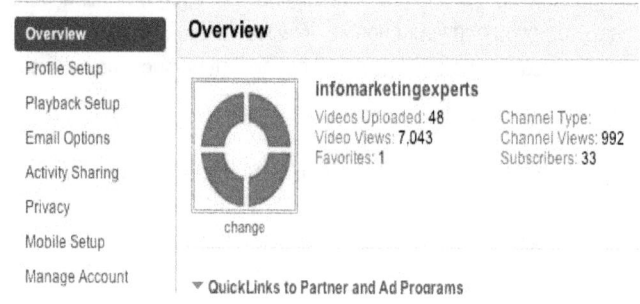

In overview, click the 'change' link to add your own image.

Just so you know, the graphic shown was created by yours truly in Adobe Photoshop.

http://www.MarcBullard.com

Analysis and Research Tools

Oddly enough, a lot of businesses large and small aren't using all of the free services YouTube offers to increase, analyze, and target traffic. I have outlined some of the most important and highly overlooked features YouTube provides for all of its members. With the knowledge you get from this section, you will be able to:

• **Search and discover popular trends**

• **Find what types of videos certain demographics of people are watching**

• **Analyze who's watching your videos**

• **Immediately create your own animations with no software, no equipment, and no money**

• **Edit videos you already have online**

• **Try out new features of YouTube before they are available**

• **Much more.**

Strangely, YouTube made a lot of these sites and features some of the hardest things to find. No buttons, confusing links, and abandoned pages* indicates that this is all relatively new technology. In researching for this book, I realized a lot of these pages are being transitioned into newer sites.

So in a way, that's cool because with this information at our fingertips, we are getting in on the ground floor of the new features. We can figure out new ways to use them and be the first kids on the block with the newest toys. That also means you should bookmark the pages to get to them quickly. Don't miss out.

*Some may argue that abandoned pages would indicate that YouTube is not interested in such features. Most of the abandoned pages come from YouTube adopting the content into another, newer page. And trust me, the abandoned pages were hard to find and very scarce.

YouTube Trends - *http://youtube-trends.blogspot.com/*

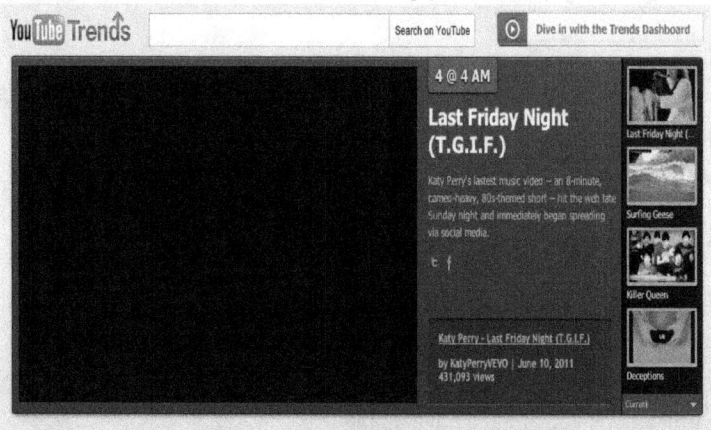

YouTube Trends is a new site created by YouTube to showcase the latest videos and trends that are currently popular on their site. YouTube Trends is made for anybody who wants to know what's popular on YouTube at any given moment. The site offers you a couple of categories that break down the information such as 'Trending Topics', 'Trending Videos', and '4 at 4'.

'**Trending Topics**' is a list of topics YouTube has found to be rising in popularity.

Trending Topics

> London Ufos

> Google Project

> Eminem Royce Da 5'9

> China Mirage Over

> Cm Punk On Raw

> Dog Like

> Glbt Gay

> The Wild Thornberrys Bad Romance Fea...

> New York America's Got Talent Auditions

Topics are determined by an algorithm and by similar keywords in titles, tags, and descriptions of videos. For example, if a lot of people are responding to protests in Egypt by creating and posting videos, a possible trending topic would be 'Egypt Protests'. You can use this to your advantage.

You could check out the latest trending topics and create a video yourself with similar keywords. If you can relate those keywords to your product or services, you could grab a lot of viewers searching those terms.

Remember, the 'Trending Topics' are updated daily, you could do this over and over again. This is just one of many ways you could use 'Trending Topics' to help your marketing.

'**Trending Videos**' is a list of currently popular videos that have been embedded on the web's most popular sites (YouTube doesn't tell you what they are) and a large number of people viewed it either on these other sites or on YouTube itself.

Trending Videos

Drunken Guy Wrecks Bathroom

UFOs Over London Friday 2011 - UFO Fleet Over...

Mike Zunino Breaks Bat

Crazy Bitch Goes OFF On Bus Driver

Soldier, Home Early, Surprises Son At High School

Harrison Ford - "30 Pages"

In addition to using the technique mentioned above with 'Trending Videos', you could also go to these videos and leave a comment or video response.

http://www.MarcBullard.com

Leaving comments and video responses on popular videos can help get traffic to your YouTube channel or website. Also, you will look like a person who's "in the know". Knowledgeable people are easier to find online and psychologically easier to buy from.

'**4 at 4**' are videos that are creating significant buzz on YouTube and other sites.

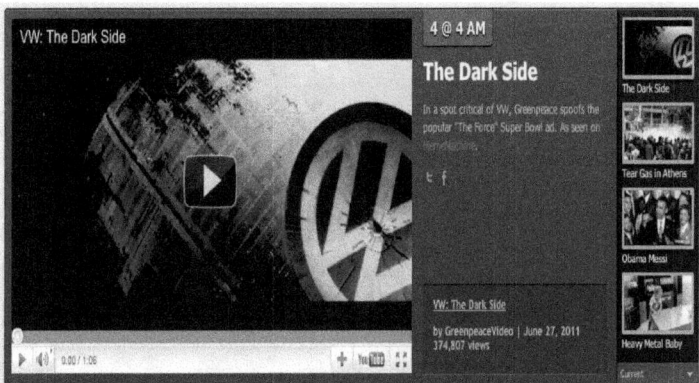

Every 4am and 4pm Eastern time, YouTube Trends identifies the top 4 videos at that time. '4 at 4' is a great way to see the most recent popular happenings at the time. This is a great way to find out what's new right away.

Using all three of these features can help you find and identify possible viral videos of the future. Discovering a viral video in the early stages is an extremely powerful way to generate traffic, if you know how to use it.

Just so you know, you can view the trending videos for each category as well.

Categories

‣ Advertising	‣ Community
‣ Culture	‣ Gaming
‣ Holidays	‣ Local
‣ Movies	‣ Music
‣ Newsroom	‣ Politics
‣ Search	‣ Sports
‣ Technology	‣ Viral
‣ Weather	‣ World

Trends Dashboard - *http://www.youtube.com/trendsdashboard*

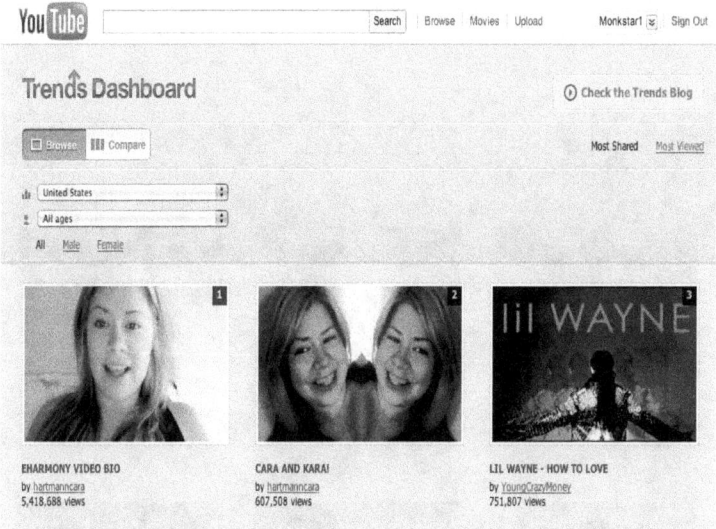

One of the best and often overlooked features of YouTube Trends is the 'Trends Dashboard'. Located at the top of the YouTube Trends website, the Dashboard opens up more tools to help you figure out a wealth of information. To access this, click the 'Dive in with the trends' button.

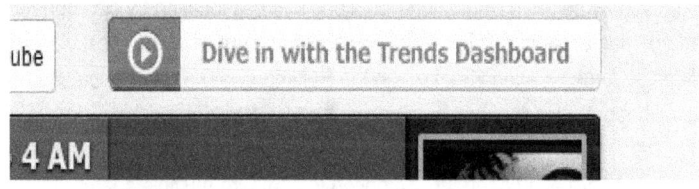

The Trends Dashboard let's you look at the most viewed and most shared videos.

You can browse them with different options such as location by city, gender, and age demographic. This means you could find out what the most viewed videos by females aged 18-24 are in the Baltimore, MD area. Or you can view what both genders are watching in the 55-64 age group.

The Dashboard even offers up the option to compare multiple search parameters.

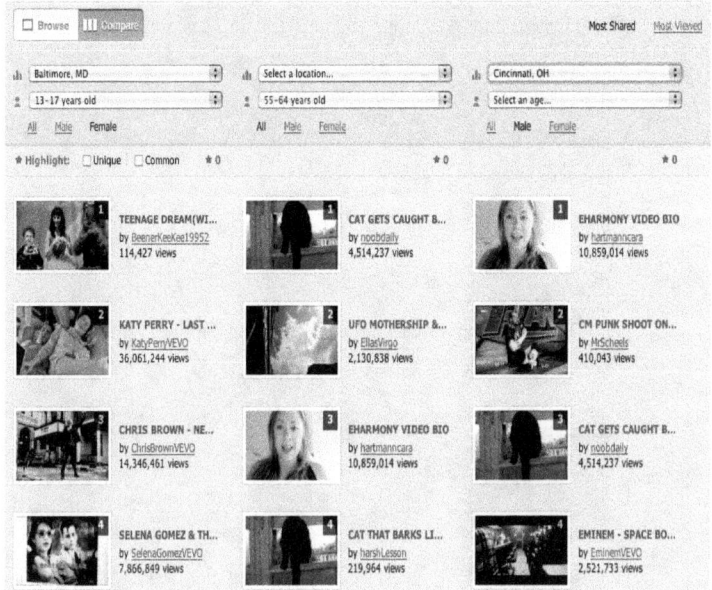

You could compare what males, aged 25-34, are watching in Cincinnati, Los Angeles, and Jacksonville. Or you could look at the same thing for females. The options are endless. Once you know what your target audience is looking for, you can create and market videos of the same type, style, length, etc.

<u>YouTube Charts</u> - *http://www.youtube.com/charts*

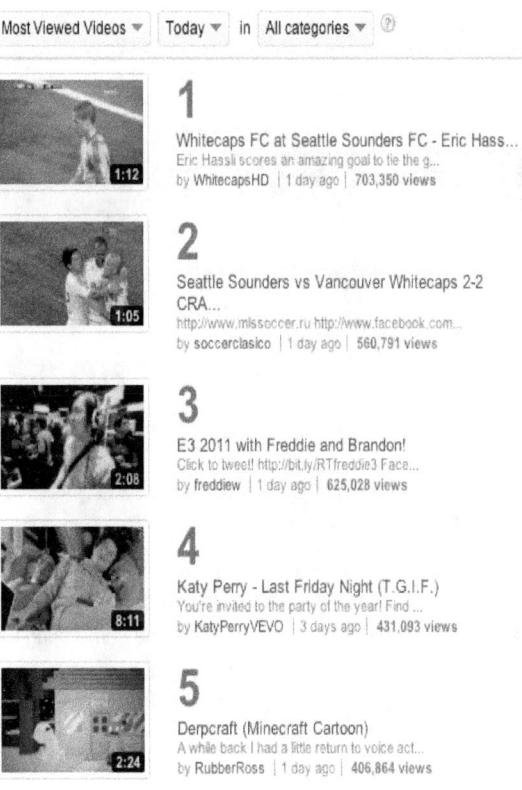

'YouTube Charts' is similar to YouTube Trends in that it provides a numbered list of the top videos in certain categories. However it differs in the fact that 'YouTube Charts' focuses on how many views and likes videos receive. 'YouTube Charts' lets you filter the results from Most Viewed, Most Liked, Top Subscribed Channel, and much more.

You can also see results for the top videos for just today, this week, this month, or of all time. It also lets you filter even more by category. You can choose any of the common categories YouTube offers you when you upload a video such as comedy, entertainment, education, how to, style, and more.

Here's another way to use 'YouTube Charts'. Find the most popular channels of the day under a category that matches your business. Then, subscribe to their channels. Subscribing to a popular channel does a couple of things for you.

First, you will now be notified if that channel uploads any more videos. This is a good way to keep tabs of what competitors are posting and talking about; it keeps you in the loop. Also, there's sort of an unspoken agreement that if you subscribe to someone's channel, they subscribe to yours. Although this isn't always the case, when it works it can build up your YouTube channel quickly, which is always important.

YouTube TestTube - *http://www.youtube.com/testtube*

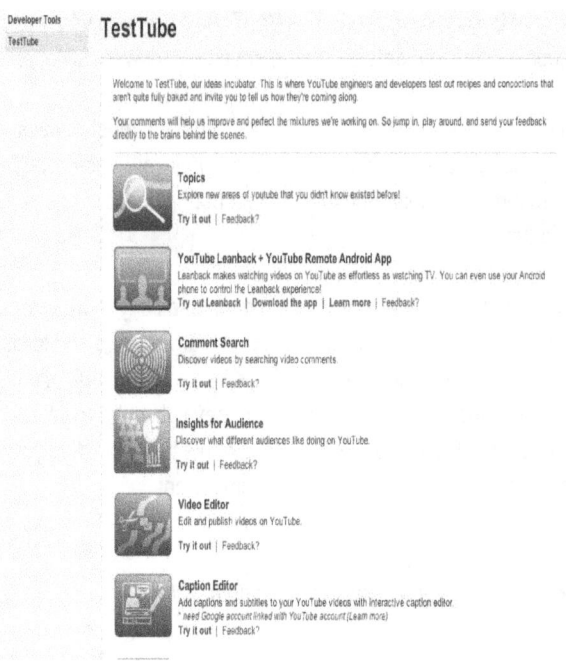

YouTube TestTube is where you can view and test some of the newest ideas developers have for YouTube. This is where they and you can try out ideas such as:

Topics - Type in a search term and YouTube will provide you with topics and subtopics that are related. When you click on a subtopic, you will see the most viewed, recently uploaded, and the option to explore further. This is a great tool to find out what your competition is doing.

Music discovery - Similar to the popular music site Pandora, music discovery lets you enter in a band name and YouTube will provide you with music videos from that artist as well as artists with the same musical style. A lot of people use YouTube for playing music. If you're in a band, uploading your songs to YouTube is a fantastic and free way to get publicity for you.

http://www.MarcBullard.com

There are other new inventions to try out at TestTube as well. It's worth checking them out. YouTube TestTube is a neat little way to play around with the features that YouTube may make standard in the future. Wouldn't it be nice to have a leg up on the competition when it comes to using these features?

Video Editor

Another feature YouTube is giving its members is a video editor. The Video Editor is a unique beast that does in fact let you make basic edits to video and add a music track, but it is lacking in some ways.

As a video editor for over 11 years now, I have to hand it to them. It was a nice effort but unfortunately they missed out on some key features that would make video editing fantastic. But enough about what it can't do, let's look at what it can do. First, let's look at the interface. The video editor is laid out with video clips, a timeline, and a few tabs with other options. The tabs are located at the top of the video editor.

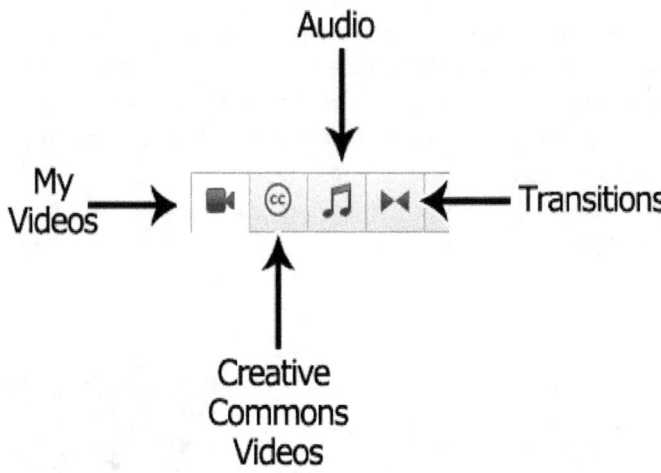

Any video that you have uploaded to YouTube is eligible for you to edit and will be seen. Nobody else has access to your videos and the same goes for you with theirs. If what you've uploaded isn't exactly what you need, there are also Creative Commons videos for you and every other YouTube user to choose from.

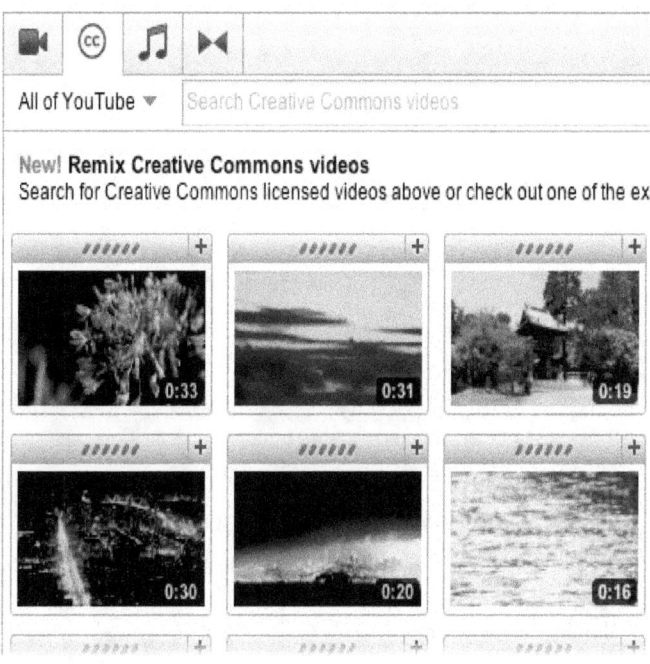

The CC videos are nice and varied with a lot of stock footage style videos.

To add an audio track, YouTube provides a large list of artists' tracks to choose from.

How popular and well known these tracks are is beyond me. I didn't recognize any artist available which means either I'm getting too old or the music selection is coming from lesser known acts. We'll go with the latter for now.

In order to start editing, simply click either one or your videos, a creative commons video, or an audio track and drag it into the timeline below.

Once you have some video clips in your video timeline, you can then trim them, rotate, and add effects such as making the shot black and white, changing the brightness, and changing the contrast. To do any fine tuning with your clip, options are available when a user hovers his mouse over any clip.

The first option (scissors) lets you edit your clip.

Basically, it lets you shorten or lengthen the video clip. Make sure you save any trimming that you do. You can also go to the other two editing options by either saving and going back to the timeline or clicking the tabs located in the top left of the trim window.

The next tab lets you rotate the image.

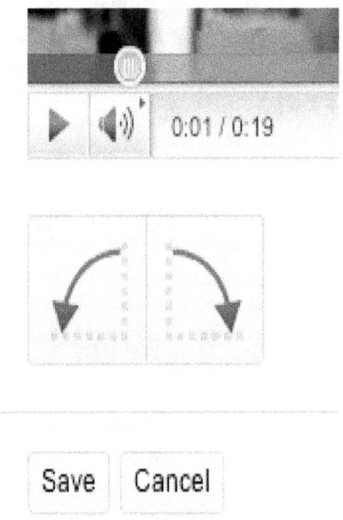

Click either arrow to rotate.

The next tab lets you add effects.

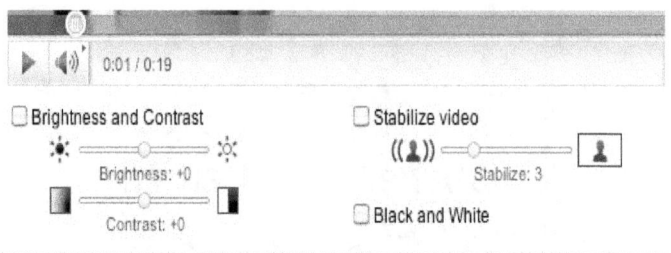

The effects - if you can call them that - let you change the brightness and contrast, stabilize the video if it's bouncy, and create a black and white image. You will only be able to view what the effects are doing either after you've saved or after the clip you're working on has started over from the beginning of the preview window again. This makes it virtually impossible to have any control over what you're doing.

The audio works pretty much the same way. Click the audio tab and find a track you like. You can even search by genre or artist.

When you find your audio track, drag that into the timeline. You can monitor the audio and effect how much is overlaid over the video's audio in the timeline.

ontent available through the YouTube Video Editor.

Finally, when you're all done you can publish your work back to your YouTube channel and have a bright, shiny new video.

If YouTube keeps improving the video editor they may have something on their hands. Until then, it's still a little too rough to work with in my opinion.

YouTube Creator's Corner - *http://www.youtube.com/t/creators_corner*

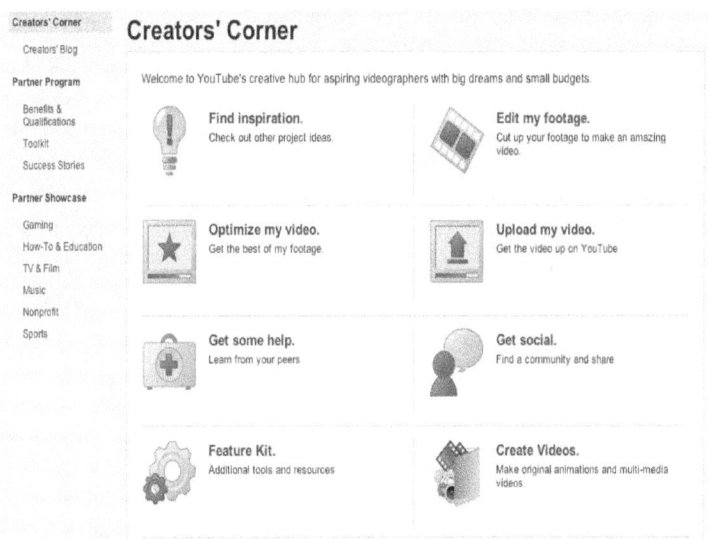

YouTube's Creators' Corner is specifically for people who make videos for YouTube. In the Creators' Corner you can get ideas from other members, get help in the community forums, find inspiration, learn about every feature of YouTube, and create your own videos.

The last option - create your own videos - is one of the most important options available to you. This is different than editing your video, this is creating one from scratch. YouTube gives you a couple of choices as to how you create your video such as:

<u>Stupeflix Video Maker</u>

<u>Xtranormal Movie Maker</u>

<u>GoAnimate</u>

<u>One True Media</u>

With these free options, you can have some videos created right there on the spot. It only takes a few minutes to make one. Go for it, give them a try. I personally like GoAnimate.

<u>Video Speed History</u> - *http://www.youtube.com/my_speed*

Want to check the speed of your video connection? Take a look at your YouTube Video Speed History. It is true, video does take longer to load than text. This tool will show you your average speed compared to other average speeds.

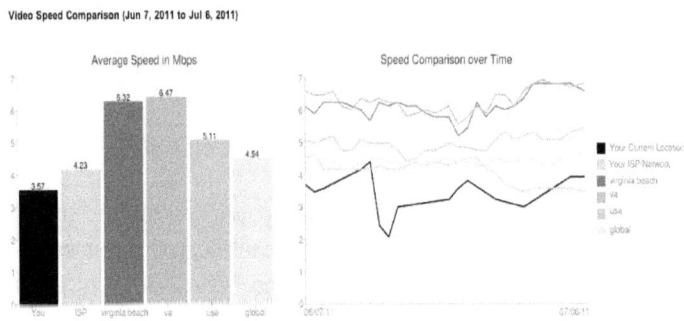

<u>Comment Search</u> - *http://www.youtube.com/comment_search*
You can even search comments for specific terms. Type in a keyword phrase that matches your niche. YouTube's Comment Search will show you

the latest comments to contain those words. Now you can go to them yourself and either leave a video response or comment.

Comment Search

	Search comments
☐ Show comments in **All** languages	

Sort by Rating | Sort by Time

How To: The Braided Top Knot 🗨

1368 👍 OMG! Blair do a room tour at your parents h

posted 6 months ago by someone12310

520 👍 omg blair you look sooo pretty with your hair

YouTube Analytics (Formerly YouTube Insight)
Attempting to get traffic, views, and comments from your videos but not tracking your efforts' progress is a huge shot in the foot. You should always be comparing and contrasting what efforts you made and what results you achieved from them. Analytics is just the tool for you.

YouTube Analytics - formerly known as Insight - is an extremely powerful set of tools that can provide you with a lot of information about your videos, your audience, and your customers.

To access Analytics, click your username in the upper right hand corner and select 'Video Manager' from the drop down list. In your video manager, there are links at the top of the page. One of them is the 'Analytics' link.

Subscriptions | Analytics (Insight) | Messages

http://www.MarcBullard.com

Clicking on 'Analytics' will bring you to the Overview page.

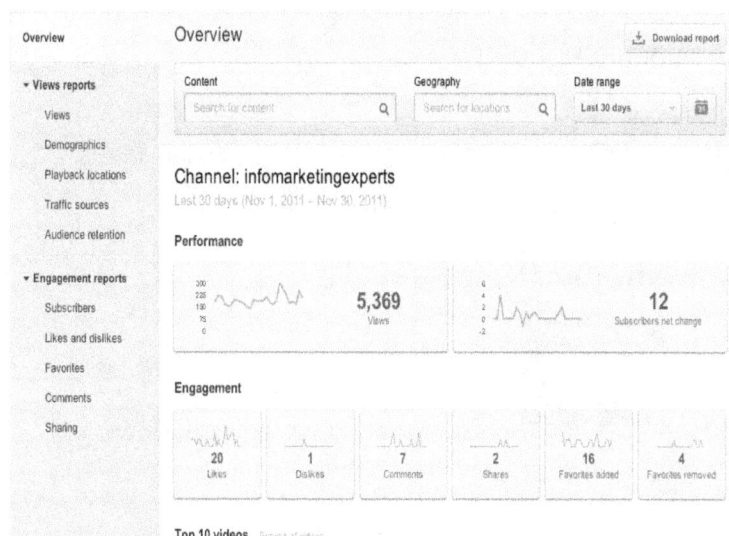

This page provides high level, general categories such as 'Performance', 'Engagement', 'Top 10 videos', 'Demographics', 'Discovery', and more. You can also view by 'Content', 'Geography', and 'Date Range'. The default date range is the last 30 days.

The large section of the Overview page will provide you with some of the most used widgets. The smaller, left hand section also contains these widgets but in a different order. This left hand section breaks down the widgets into two larger sections: **Views reports** and **Engagement reports**.

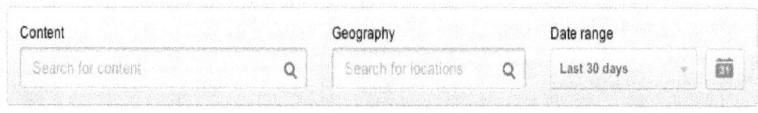

Data Filters are available for all reports. This lets you search for content, such as a specific video; geography, such as a certain country; or by date range. You can check these numbers by daily, weekly, monthly, yearly, or custom metrics. Using data filters will change the results on your overview page.

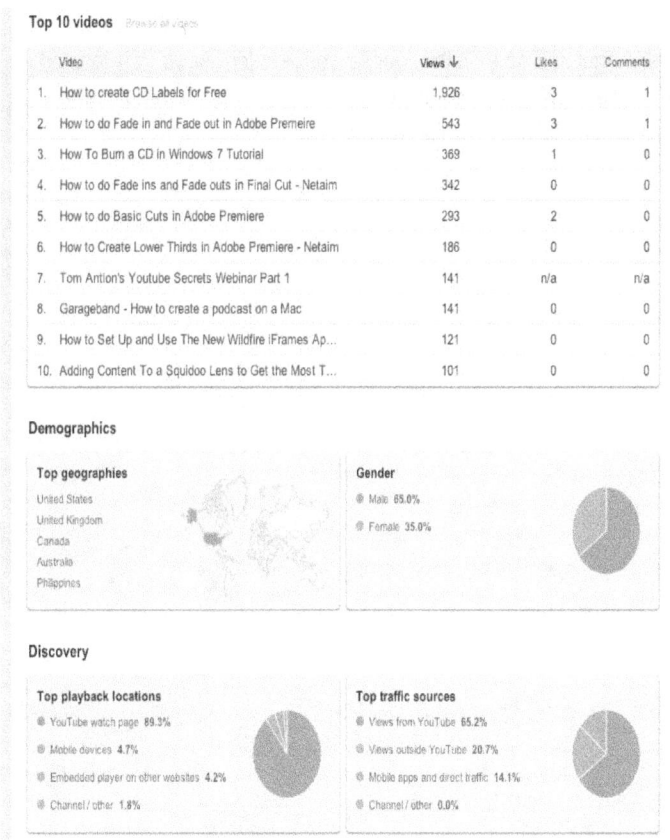

Top 10 videos   Browse all videos

Video	Views ↓	Likes	Comments
1. How to create CD Labels for Free	1,926	3	1
2. How to do Fade in and Fade out in Adobe Premeire	543	3	1
3. How To Burn a CD in Windows 7 Tutorial	369	1	0
4. How to do Fade ins and Fade outs in Final Cut - Netaim	342	0	0
5. How to do Basic Cuts in Adobe Premiere	293	2	0
6. How to Create Lower Thirds in Adobe Premiere - Netaim	186	0	0
7. Tom Antion's Youtube Secrets Webinar Part 1	141	n/a	n/a
8. Garageband - How to create a podcast on a Mac	141	0	0
9. How to Set Up and Use The New Wildfire iFrames Ap...	121	0	0
10. Adding Content To a Squidoo Lens to Get the Most T...	101	0	0

Demographics

Top geographies
United States
United Kingdom
Canada
Australia
Philippines

Gender
Male 65.0%
Female 35.0%

Discovery

Top playback locations
YouTube watch page 89.3%
Mobile devices 4.7%
Embedded player on other websites 4.2%
Channel / other 1.8%

Top traffic sources
Views from YouTube 65.2%
Views outside YouTube 20.7%
Mobile apps and direct traffic 14.1%
Channel / other 0.0%

Each section - called widgets - is click-able. When you click on a widget, you get your reports for that section.

http://www.MarcBullard.com

Also, every report that is provided to you is available to download for your records. Once clicked, you will receive a .csv file you can keep in a spreadsheet or print out.

The first widget available on the overview page is for 'Views'. It is located under a larger **Performance** category. Clicking on the 'Views' widget will bring up more details concerning your views.

You will be able to see your videos listed by views as well as geographical information and dates. In order to access geographical information or dates, click on the corresponding tab.

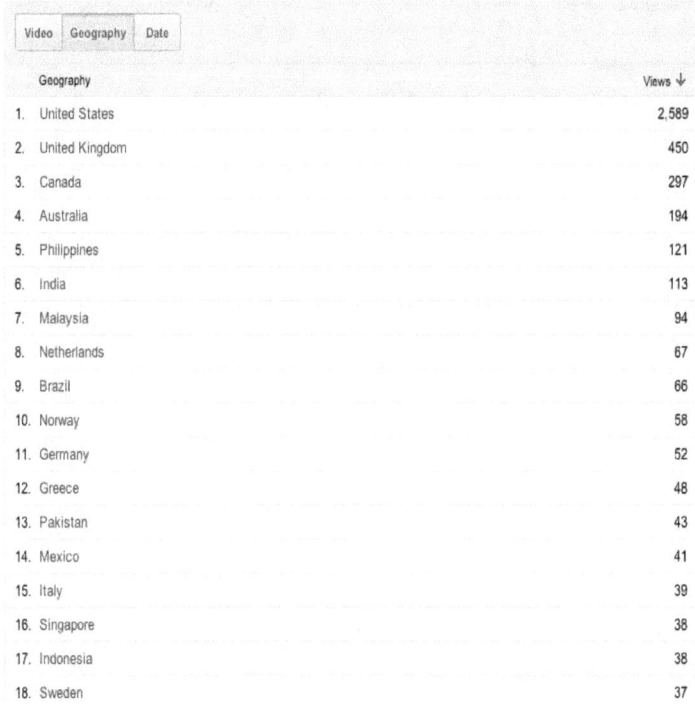

	Geography	Views ↓
1.	United States	2,589
2.	United Kingdom	450
3.	Canada	297
4.	Australia	194
5.	Philippines	121
6.	India	113
7.	Malaysia	94
8.	Netherlands	67
9.	Brazil	66
10.	Norway	58
11.	Germany	52
12.	Greece	48
13.	Pakistan	43
14.	Mexico	41
15.	Italy	39
16.	Singapore	38
17.	Indonesia	38
18.	Sweden	37

Geography tab.

Video	Geography	Date		
Date ↓				Views
1. Nov 28, 2011				205
2. Nov 27, 2011				251
3. Nov 26, 2011				165
4. Nov 25, 2011				182
5. Nov 24, 2011				171
6. Nov 23, 2011				227
7. Nov 22, 2011				266
8. Nov 21, 2011				299
9. Nov 20, 2011				187
10. Nov 19, 2011				163
11. Nov 18, 2011				177
12. Nov 17, 2011				212
13. Nov 16, 2011				187
14. Nov 15, 2011				185
15. Nov 14, 2011				186
16. Nov 13, 2011				193
17. Nov 12, 2011				136
18. Nov 11, 2011				148
19. Nov 10, 2011				171

Date tab.

All of these results are important to pay attention to. First, you can use this information to determine what countries are interested in your video. If you find that more people are watching your video from Brazil, it might make sense to translate your captions or transcript into Portuguese; thereby capturing an even larger audience from that country. You should also pay attention to the dates that views either increase or decrease. Of course views are going to fluctuate, but if you notice a large difference between particular days you may want to make a note of anything that could have caused that large fluctuation, such as whether it was a weekend, holiday, you made a change in tags on that day, etc.

Not only can you see your views with a line graph, you can also see them by geographical location. Clicking the 'Map' button will provide you with a map of the world. Holding your mouse over any area will give you the number of views that came from that area.

*In Russia, views count **you**!*

The next widget under the **Performance** category is for 'Subscribers net change'. This is the change in total subscribers found by subtracting subscribers you lost from the subscribers you gained in that selected date or region.

Subscribers gained - Subscribers lost = Subscribers net change

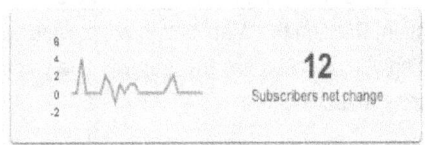

Clicking this widget will show you the 'Subscribers net change', 'Subscribers gained', and 'Subscribers lost' reports.

Just like with other widgets, you have data filters, options for either a line graph or map, and ways to sort by 'Video', 'Geography', or 'Date'. Also,

http://www.MarcBullard.com

individually clicking on the 'Subscribers net change', 'Subscribers gained', or 'Subscribers lost' widgets will bring up information related to only that widget.

It is important to look at what videos are getting subscribers. You may also see one of the options as 'Channel / other'. This means there wasn't any particular video that got a subscriber; but you got one nonetheless.

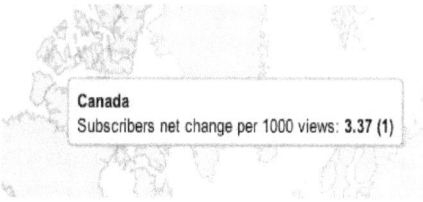

One other important thing to know is if you search your subscribers using the 'Map' option, the results will show a number based on 1000 views.

You can change these settings by clicking the drop down box on the right side of the map widget.

Back on the 'Overview' page, you will see widgets for the **Engagement** category. Engagement widgets cover 'Likes', 'Dislikes', 'Comments', 'Shares', 'Favorites added', and 'Favorites removed'.

Engagement

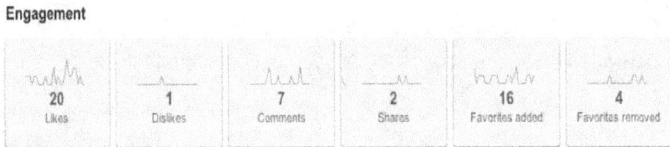

Clicking the 'Likes' widget will bring you to that report page.

Channel: infomarketingexperts

Last 30 days (Nov 2, 2011 – Dec 1, 2011)

Total ratings	Likes	Dislikes
22	21	1

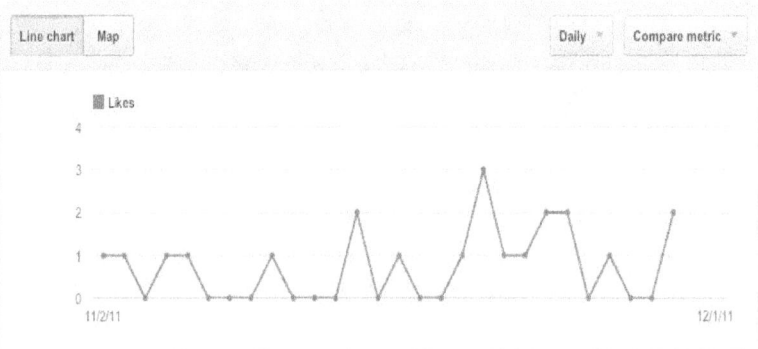

| Line chart | Map | | Daily ▾ | Compare metric ▾ |

Likes

4
3
2
1
0

11/2/11   12/1/11

| Video | Geography | Date |

	Video	Total ratings ↓	Likes	Dislikes	Likes / Dislikes
1.	How to create CD…	3	3	0	
2.	How to do Fade in…	3	3	0	
3.	Viral Video - Clos…	2	2	0	
4.	Good Example of …	2	2	0	
5.	How to do Basic …	2	2	0	
6.	How To Burn a C…	1	1	0	
7.	How To Create A …	1	1	0	
8.	How to Use Keyw…	1	1	0	

This report page has all of the same options as 'Views', 'Subscribers', and others, so there's no needto go over every option you can use. However, there is one metric that hasn't been covered yet, and that is the 'Compare metric'.

http://www.MarcBullard.com

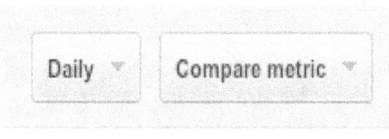

The 'Compare metric' will let you see extra information displayed on your line chart. It's not available for every report, but for the reports that do have it, the metric will be a little different.

Compare metric for 'Likes' and 'Dislikes'.

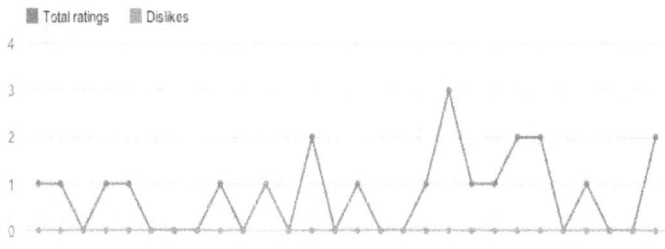

Choosing a compare metric will display extra information.

You can see reports and their compare metrics for your entire YouTube channel or for individual videos.

On the Overview page, below the **Engagement** category, you will see a list of your **Top 10 Videos.**

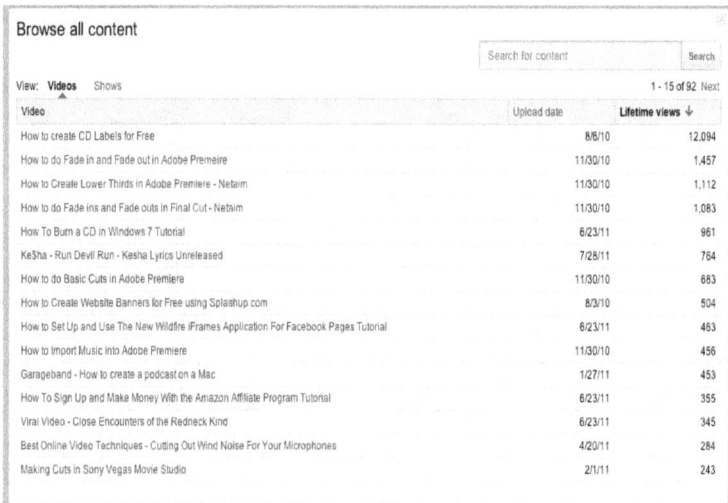

Top 10 videos Browse all videos

	Video	Views ↓	Likes	Comments
1.	How to create CD Labels for Free	1,956	3	2
2.	How to do Fade in and Fade out in Adobe Premeire	555	3	1
3.	How To Burn a CD in Windows 7 Tutorial	362	1	0
4.	How to do Fade ins and Fade outs in Final Cut - Netaim	346	0	0
5.	How to do Basic Cuts in Adobe Premiere	303	2	0
6.	How to Create Lower Thirds in Adobe Premiere - Netaim	183	0	0
7.	Tom Antion's Youtube Secrets Webinar Part 1	145	1	0
8.	Garageband - How to create a podcast on a Mac	136	0	0
9.	How to Set Up and Use The New Wildfire iFrames Ap...	123	0	0
10.	Adding Content To a Squidoo Lens to Get the Most T...	99	0	0

The top 10 videos are listed in order of views. You can also choose to browse all of your videos.

Browse all content

Search for content   Search

View: **Videos** Shows   1 - 15 of 92 Next

Video	Upload date	Lifetime views ↓
How to create CD Labels for Free	8/6/10	12,094
How to do Fade in and Fade out in Adobe Premeire	11/30/10	1,457
How to Create Lower Thirds in Adobe Premiere - Netaim	11/30/10	1,112
How to do Fade ins and Fade outs in Final Cut - Netaim	11/30/10	1,083
How To Burn a CD in Windows 7 Tutorial	6/23/11	961
Ke$ha - Run Devil Run - Kesha Lyrics Unreleased	7/28/11	764
How to do Basic Cuts in Adobe Premiere	11/30/10	683
How to Create Website Banners for Free using Splashup.com	8/3/10	504
How to Set Up and Use The New Wildfire iFrames Application For Facebook Pages Tutorial	6/23/11	463
How to Import Music into Adobe Premiere	11/30/10	456
Garageband - How to create a podcast on a Mac	1/27/11	453
How To Sign Up and Make Money With the Amazon Affiliate Program Tutorial	6/23/11	355
Viral Video - Close Encounters of the Redneck Kind	6/23/11	345
Best Online Video Techniques - Cutting Out Wind Noise For Your Microphones	4/20/11	284
Making Cuts in Sony Vegas Movie Studio	2/1/11	243

When browsing all of your content, you can arrange the results by 'Upload date' or 'Lifetime views'. Clicking on any title of a video will give you an overview page for only that video.

Below the **Top 10 videos** category is the **Demographics** category.

Clicking the 'Top geographies' widget will show you what countries are providing the most views. A list of the countries in order of views will also be available.

Line chart | Map

0 — 2603

1.	United States	2,603
2.	United Kingdom	456
3.	Canada	298
4.	Australia	193
5.	Philippines	124
6.	India	116
7.	Malaysia	92
8.	Netherlands	70
9.	Brazil	66
10.	Norway	58
11.	Germany	56
12.	Greece	47
13.	Pakistan	42
14.	Italy	42
15.	Singapore	41
16.	Indonesia	38
17.	Sweden	37
18.	Romania	36
19.	Mexico	36
20.	Poland	35
21.	Thailand	33
22.	Hong Kong	33
23.	Ireland	33
24.	Portugal	32

Clicking on the name of a country will show you information on only that country.

Clicking the 'Video' tab for that country will show you the exact videos that received views from that country.

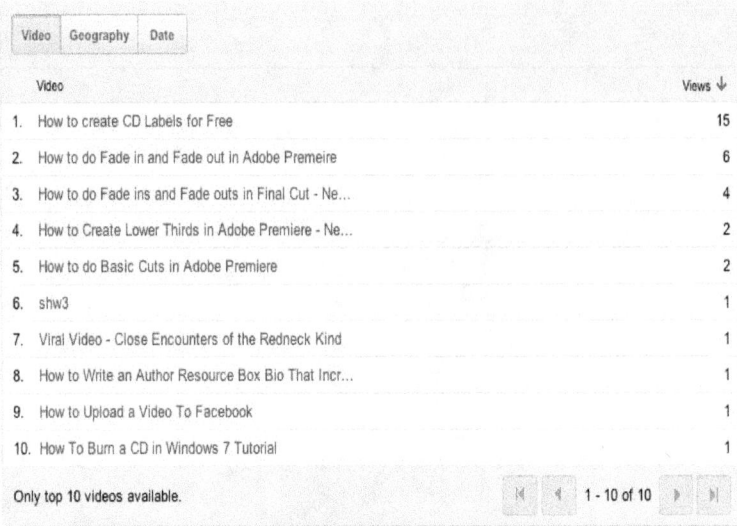

If you find a country that likes a particular video, you may want to create one tailored specifically for that country, or at least add transcripts in that country's language to increase even more views.

The next widget located under the **Demographics** category is for gender.

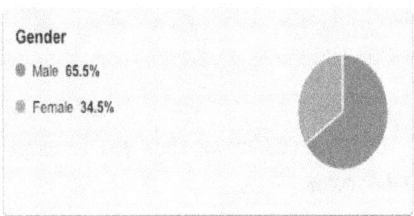

Clicking on this widget will provide you with gender, age, and location information about your viewers.

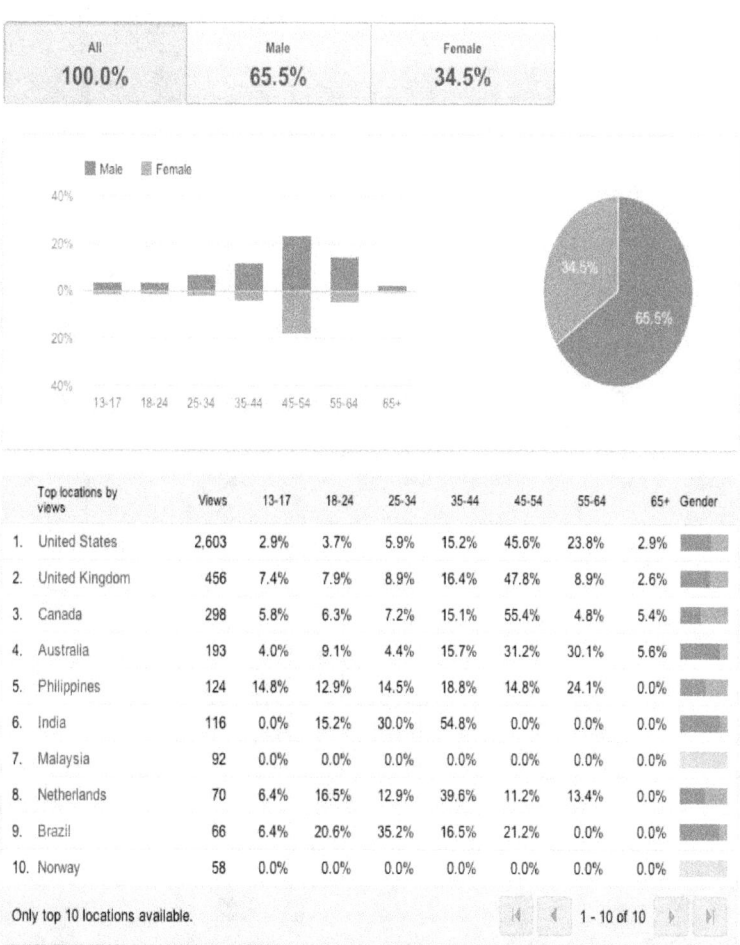

All	Male	Female
100.0%	65.5%	34.5%

Top locations by views		Views	13-17	18-24	25-34	35-44	45-54	55-64	65+	Gender
1.	United States	2,603	2.9%	3.7%	5.9%	15.2%	45.6%	23.8%	2.9%	
2.	United Kingdom	456	7.4%	7.9%	8.9%	16.4%	47.8%	8.9%	2.6%	
3.	Canada	298	5.8%	6.3%	7.2%	15.1%	55.4%	4.8%	5.4%	
4.	Australia	193	4.0%	9.1%	4.4%	15.7%	31.2%	30.1%	5.6%	
5.	Philippines	124	14.8%	12.9%	14.5%	18.8%	14.8%	24.1%	0.0%	
6.	India	116	0.0%	15.2%	30.0%	54.8%	0.0%	0.0%	0.0%	
7.	Malaysia	92	0.0%	0.0%	0.0%	0.0%	0.0%	0.0%	0.0%	
8.	Netherlands	70	6.4%	16.5%	12.9%	39.6%	11.2%	13.4%	0.0%	
9.	Brazil	66	6.4%	20.6%	35.2%	16.5%	21.2%	0.0%	0.0%	
10.	Norway	58	0.0%	0.0%	0.0%	0.0%	0.0%	0.0%	0.0%	

Only top 10 locations available.   1 - 10 of 10

Pay attention to this information. If you have a particular video that is getting a lot of attention from a specific gender, location, or age group, you may want to create more videos like that one. Also, if you have a product or service that fits a specific demographic, this will let you know what videos are reaching your desired audience.

http://www.MarcBullard.com

The **Discovery** category contains two very useful widgets, 'Top playback locations' and 'Top traffic sources'.

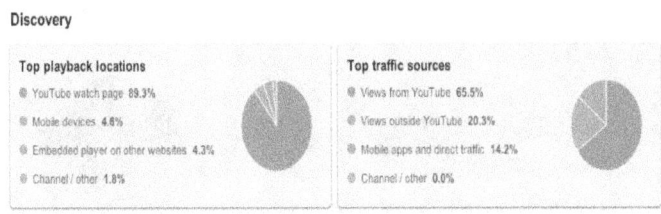

'Top playback locations' will show you a graph and information on your views and where they are coming from.

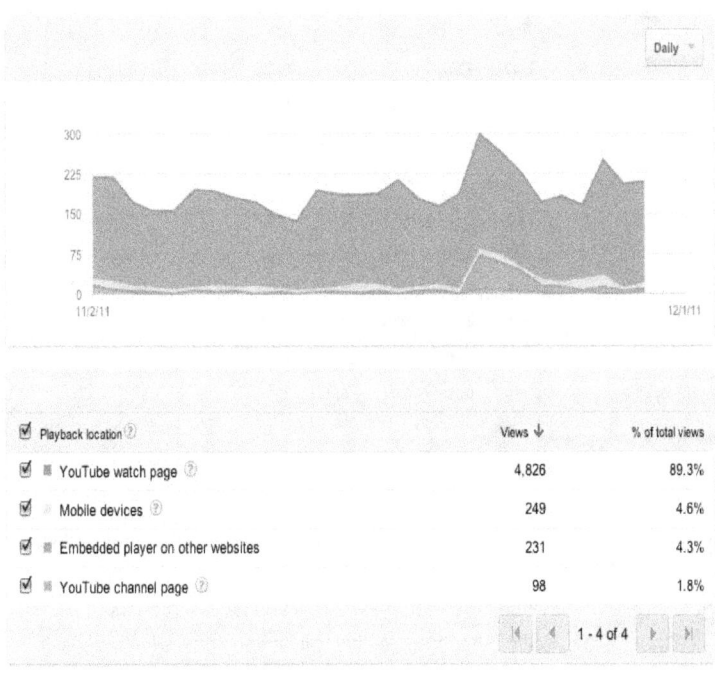

The Playback location will tell you where your views are coming from. The location entitled "Embedded player on other websites" won't tell you what the other sites are unless you are looking at the locations for specific videos.

Playback location for a specific video.

If you look at the Playback location reports for a specific video, you can click on the "Embedded player on other websites" link to see where that video is embedded.

Looking at the other websites your video is embedded on will let you know exactly where your video is playing. Also, you may find sites that you could contact and try to send more videos to, or offer other options such as submitting articles for them or placing a banner ad on their site. This can increase traffic to your site and increase sales of your products.

The 'Top traffic sources' widget is also very helpful, it is located under the **Discovery** category.

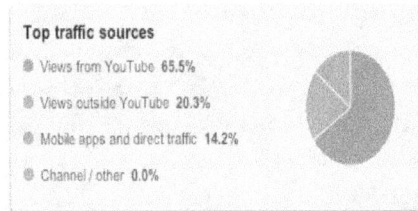

This widget will show you how people discovered your video. There's many ways people find videos: they search for them on YouTube, Google, or other search engines; they click on Suggested videos, or they can follow links from social networking sites such as Twitter or Facebook.

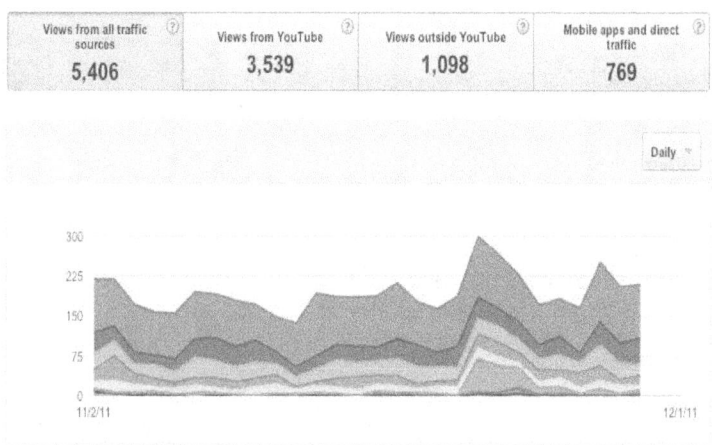

Views from all traffic sources	Views from YouTube	Views outside YouTube	Mobile apps and direct traffic
5,406	3,539	1,098	769

Traffic source	Views ↓	% of total views
YouTube suggested video	2,523	46.7%
YouTube search	915	16.9%
Google search	752	13.9%
Mobile apps and direct traffic (unknown sources)	538	9.9%
External website	346	6.4%
Embedded player (unknown sources)	231	4.3%
YouTube features	67	1.2%
YouTube channel page	28	0.5%
YouTube subscription modules	4	0.1%
YouTube featured video	2	0.0%

Traffic sources for entire channel.

The traffic sources can be displayed for either your whole channel or individual videos. Individual videos will provide you with even more information.

http://www.MarcBullard.com

Traffic source ⑦	Views ↓	% of total views
■ YouTube suggested video	710	36.3%
▨ Google search	522	26.7%
■ YouTube search	328	16.8%
▨ External website	284	14.5%
■ Mobile apps and direct traffic (unknown sources) ⑦	182	9.3%
▨ YouTube features	16	0.8%
▨ Embedded player (unknown sources) ⑦	5	0.3%
■ YouTube channel page ⑦	2	0.1%

Traffic sources for individual videos. Note: 'YouTube suggested video' and other links are now click-able.

When you look at traffic sources for individual videos, some of those sources will be click-able. If it is available for your particular video, the 'YouTube suggested video' link is extremely useful.

		Show top level
Traffic source ⑦	Views ↓	% of total views
How to make a CD cover ⬚	124	6.3%
■ Design & print your own CD Label & Cover: Mixtape/D...	101	5.2%
How To Create CD Labels ⬚	90	4.6%
Photoshop-Tutorial - CD-Label erstellen ⬚	41	2.1%
How to print DVD/CD labels ⬚	22	1.1%
How To Create A Disk Label ⬚	21	1.1%
Mac CD/DVD Label Maker, CD. DVD Label Software f...	21	1.1%
Free DVD / CD Cover Editor for Mac OS X ⬚	21	1.1%
■ How to create CD Labels for Free ⬚	18	0.9%
■ How to use Cd Cover/Labal Tamplet with Photoshop ⬚	17	0.9%

Clicking on this link will show you other people's videos that had yours in the suggested videos column on the right hand side of YouTube.

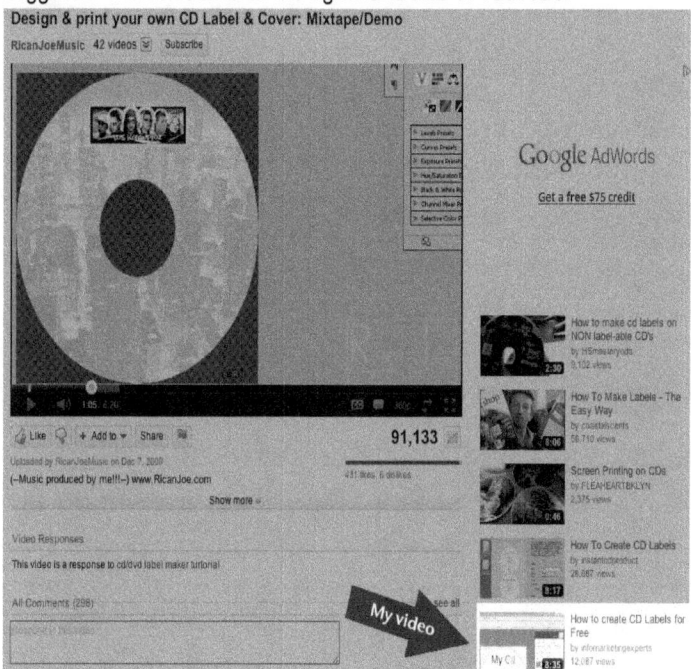

This means people went to this video first, then saw mine in the suggested videos column and clicked on that. If I want to increase my views from this other person's video, I might go and add comments or video responses to their video, possibly even suggesting to others that they will find additional or helpful information in my video. I can do this for every video that shows up in my traffic source list.

Your traffic source list may show that you got views from Google or YouTube search as well.

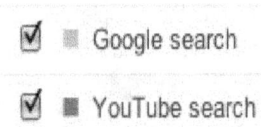

☑ ▦ Google search

☑ ■ YouTube search

Clicking on these links will provide you with a list of search terms people typed in that resulted in them clicking your video.

☑ how to make cd labels	80	4.1%
☑ making cd labels	37	1.9%
☑ cd labels free	28	1.4%
☑ how to make a cd label	26	1.3%
☑ make cd labels	23	1.2%
☑ how to make cd covers	21	1.1%
☑ how to make cd label	19	1.0%
☑ make cd labels free	17	0.9%
☑ create cd labels	17	0.9%
☑ create cd labels free	16	0.8%
☑ make a cd label	13	0.7%
☑ how to make labels for cds	12	0.6%
☑ how to create cd labels	9	0.5%
☑ make free cd labels	7	0.4%
☑ free cd labels	7	0.4%

You can look at these search terms and get ideas for other videos (or articles) you may want to create in the future. Creating more content with these search terms will show you as an expert in your field, adding credibility to your business and getting additional views as well.

Conclusion

http://www.MarcBullard.com

That's all of the features of YouTube's analytics. Don't let it scare you, it is provided to help you and your business. Poke around all of the features and use this guide to help you pinpoint where, how, and why you're getting views. Then make more videos and do it all over again, probably with better results, thanks to the information you now know how to get and use.

Video statistics button - Get information on your competition

The video statistics button is another nice, free feature YouTube has given us to use. Most people either don't know about it or don't know how to use it. The button is located to the right of the view count.

When you click on this button, a graph showing Total views appears. Below the Total views, there are Ratings, Comments, and Favorite graphs. And below those, there is a list of 'Significant discovery events'.

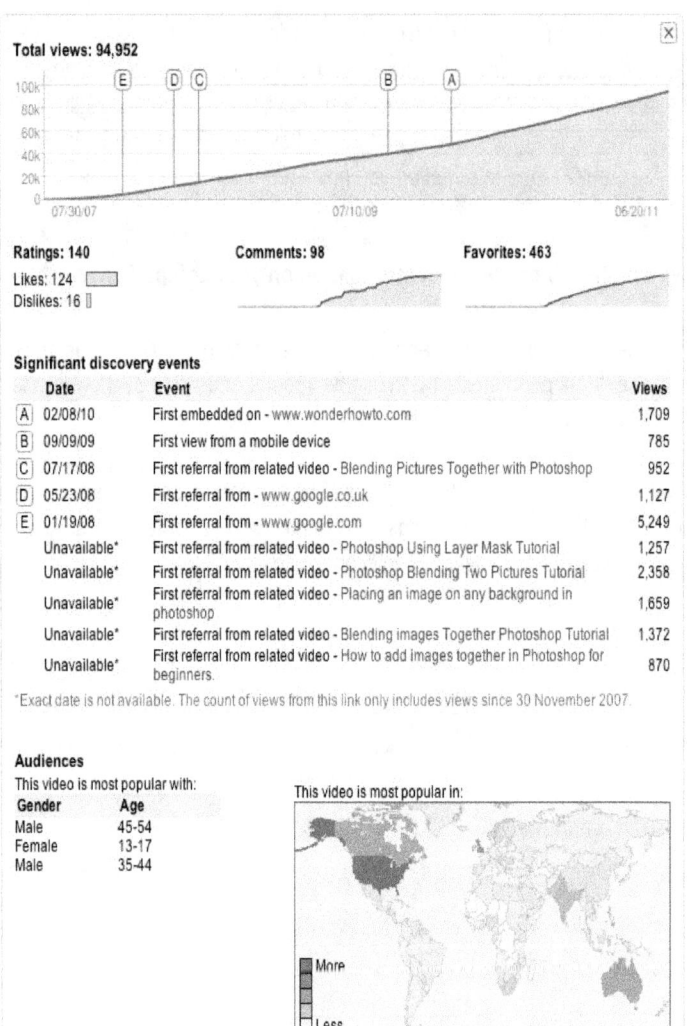

Total views: 94,952

Ratings: 140   Comments: 98   Favorites: 463

Likes: 124
Dislikes: 16

Significant discovery events

	Date	Event	Views
A	02/08/10	First embedded on - www.wonderhowto.com	1,709
B	09/09/09	First view from a mobile device	785
C	07/17/08	First referral from related video - Blending Pictures Together with Photoshop	952
D	05/23/08	First referral from - www.google.co.uk	1,127
E	01/19/08	First referral from - www.google.com	5,249
	Unavailable*	First referral from related video - Photoshop Using Layer Mask Tutorial	1,257
	Unavailable*	First referral from related video - Photoshop Blending Two Pictures Tutorial	2,358
	Unavailable*	First referral from related video - Placing an image on any background in photoshop	1,659
	Unavailable*	First referral from related video - Blending images Together Photoshop Tutorial	1,372
	Unavailable*	First referral from related video - How to add images together in Photoshop for beginners.	870

*Exact date is not available. The count of views from this link only includes views since 30 November 2007.

Audiences

This video is most popular with:

Gender	Age
Male	45-54
Female	13-17
Male	35-44

This video is most popular in:

More

Less

Under the 'Significant discovery events' is a map showing the location of viewers as well as a breakdown of what gender and age this video is most popular with.

http://www.MarcBullard.com

If you take a look at the 'Significant discovery events' you can see when and where it was first embedded (www.wonderhowto.com) and the amount of views that the embedded video has received. If this were a competitor's video or simply a video that covers the same subjects yours, you could now go to WonderHowTo.com and see if you can get your video embedded there as well.

Next on the list you can see the first time it was viewed on a mobile device. The number of views might be small but that doesn't mean you should rule out mobile. I have a feeling those numbers will grow a lot in the upcoming years.

There's also significant events below that highlight where the video was referred. Knowing these referred videos is a great way to find out where your traffic is coming from. After I knew what videos referred my video, I'd go to that video and leave a comment or video comment. Doing this can help get my video seen by more people; especially since they are looking for the same type of information as the referral video. The significant discovery events also indicate if the video came from a YouTube search as well as the keywords that got the viewers there.

12/06/07	First referral from YouTube search - photoshop masking tutorial	3,940
Unavailable*	First referral from YouTube search - photoshop mask tutorial	2,045
Unavailable*	First referral from YouTube search - photoshop masks	1,591
Unavailable*	First referral from YouTube search - photoshop mask	8,122
Unavailable*	First referral from YouTube search - photoshop masking	3,207

Analyzing what keywords got what viewers is a great technique to find other keyword phrases to use in your own videos. Here's how I would use the video statistics button:

First, I would search YouTube to find videos with some of the same keywords I use. I would then click the 'Show video statistics' button. I would then look at the significant discovery events to see what sites this video is

http://www.MarcBullard.com

embedded on. I would go to these sites and see if there's a way to get my video embedded there. Then I would look again at the significant discovery events to find if there were any related videos referring this one. I would go to all of the related videos and post a comment or video response there.

After that, I'd look at what terms came up under referrals for YouTube search and make sure I put some of them in the tags of my videos, but only if they're relevant. If I wanted to take it further, I could look at the demographics of the audience or the most popular locations (or both) and create a video specifically tailored to that demographic.

Using the 'Show video statistics' button will not only allow you to keep track of what other videos are doing, it can point you in the right direction to get traffic and find suitable keywords.

As Seen On

The 'As Seen On' feature lets viewers know where a video is embedded. This means that if you have your own video embedded on a site with high traffic, the 'As seen on' section would mention your site.

2,123,973

42,899 likes, 4,484 dislikes

As Seen On:
Funny Pictures

Viewers can click on this link and it will take them to a source page. This source page shows the viewer other videos that are embedded on the same website.

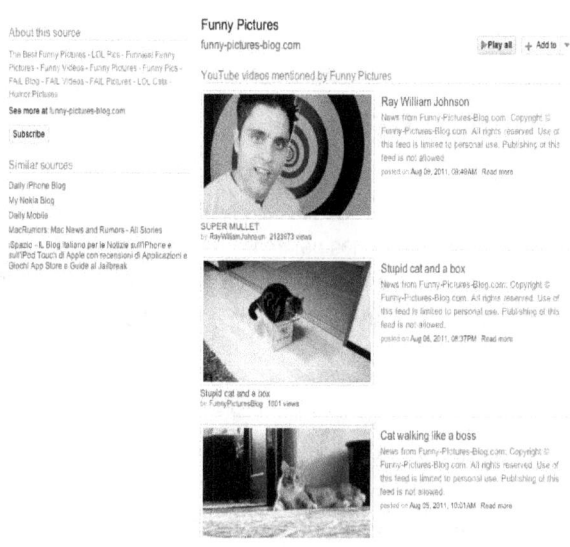

The source page will also show other sites that are similar.

Similar sources

Daily iPhone Blog

My Nokia Blog

Daily Mobile

MacRumors: Mac News and Rumors - All Stories

iSpazio - IL Blog Italiano per le Notizie sull'iPhone e sull'iPod Touch di Apple con recensioni di Applicazioni e Giochi App Store e Guide al Jailbreak

From here, the viewer can click out to any of these sites or watch other videos. As of right now, this is only available with videos that are getting a lot of traffic or with major websites; but don't let that discourage you. If you are watching a video created by your competition and you see they have an 'As seen on' link, you can go to that site and see if they will embed your video as well. This is a great way to get more traffic.

http://www.MarcBullard.com

Cool Bonus Sites

There are a few websites that I use to really beef up the exposure of my video other than what's mentioned before in this book. These are just a few of the free services that are easy to use and can save you time, get you more clicks to your website, and spread your video out over the web farther.

Annotations to your own site
If you read the section on annotations, you might remember that annotations can only link to other YouTube related sites such as your channel, a search term, or another video. There is a nice way around that problem with the site LinkedTube.

LinkedTube takes your video and lets you put an annotation on it that you provide the link to. The annotation also has a rollover feature that you can choose to use that provides a nice added graphic to the annotation. Check it out:

Video Links For YouTube™

Make Money Online Videos
Step-by-step videos show how to
make easy money online with Free
Trials

Get Paid To Party!
Learn to Make Money Promoting
Parties Like The Pros!

LinkedTube lets you create links from your YouTube™ videos.

Create video product listings, advertisements, music promotions and More.

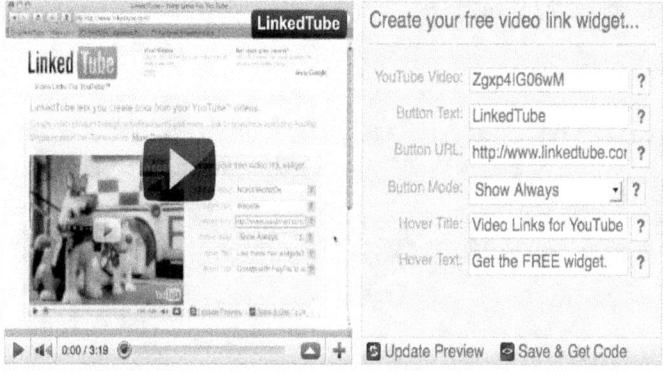

LinkedTube is completely free, you don't even have to download anything. It's all online and it's very easy.

The first thing you will need is your video's ID number. In YouTube, go to your 'Videos' and select which one you want to use. Click on the title or thumbnail to view the video. The code you need is located in the URL. The URL is the bit of code located in your Internet browser's address bar.

http://www.youtube.com/watch?v=QDETjGddab8

You don't need the entire URL, all you need is the set of letters and numbers preceding the equals (=) sign.

http://www.MarcBullard.com

You
Tube http://www.youtube.com/watch?v=QDETjGddab8

Copy this last set of letters and numbers. Now go back to LinkedTube. In the form, paste this code in the 'YouTube Video' box. Now LinkTube knows what video you want to use.

Create your free video link widget...

YouTube Video:	QDETjGddab8	?
Button Text:	YouTube Marketing Han	?
Button URL:	http://www.marcbullard.c	?
Button Mode:	Show Always ▲▼	?
Hover Title:	Get the Book	?
Hover Text:	It's Awesome	?

🔄 Update Preview   ✎ Save & Get Code

The next option is the Button Text. This will be the text on the button that your viewers will see.

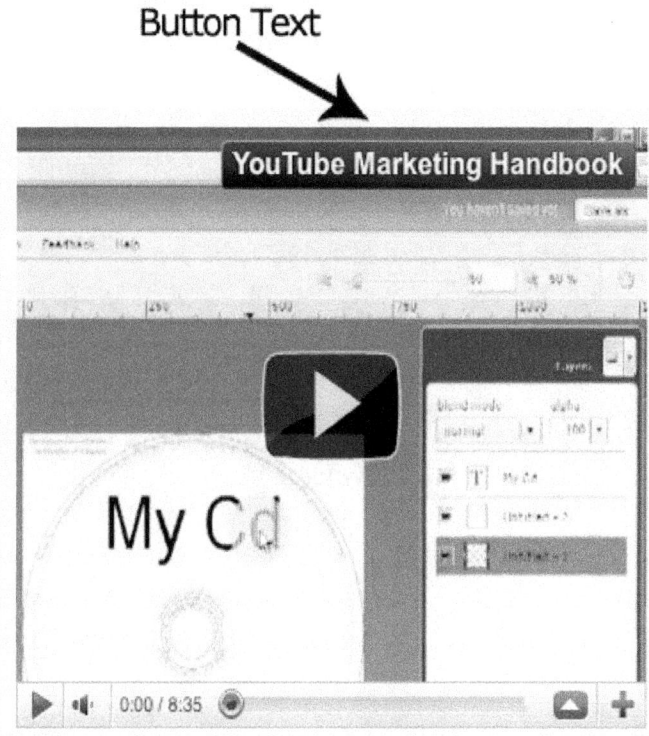

The next thing you can change is the 'Button URL'. The URL will be the link that goes to whatever page you want the people to go to when they click the button. Type this in now. Remember to put the whole entire URL. It should look like this:

http://www.yoursite.com

Where it says 'yoursite', you would put your own site.

The next option is used to determine if you want the button to be on your screen the whole time, only on when the user hovers his mouse over the button, or never. There is no reason to ever use the 'never' option.

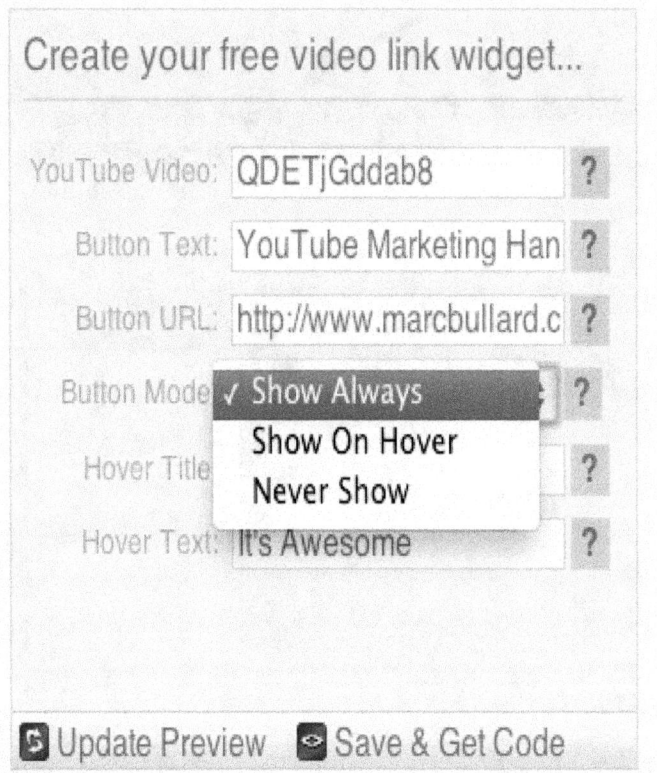

After you've determined your button mode, you can choose if you want text to show up when somebody hovers over the button. Simply type into the box whatever you want or leave it blank if you don't want anything to show up. Whatever you choose, it'll look like this:

After you enter your 'Hover Title', you have the option to enter 'Hover Text'. This is just another place to put more text if you decide to; again, leave it blank if you don't want anything there.

In order to see changes to the preview screen, be sure to click 'Update Preview' any time you enter info in the boxes. Once you have entered in all of the information, click 'Save & Get Code'.

LinkedTube will then provide you with your embed code and a few other links. The only thing you need to be concerned with is the actual embed code.

Button Link [Copy & Paste URL if PopUp Was Blocked] X

http://www.linkedtube.com

Permanent Link

http://www.linkedtube.com/Zgxp4IG06wM4eeaf0c8f581|

Embed Code

```
<object classid="clsid:d27cdb6e-ae6d-11cf-96b8-44455
<param name="movie" value="http://www.linkedtube.co
<param name="quality" value="high" />
<param name="menu" value="false" />
<embed src="http://www.linkedtube.com/static/flash/pla
</object>
```

Powered by LinkedTube.com

All you need to do is select all of the text in the 'Embed Code' box and then copy it. Then, you need to paste this code on your website page or blog post.

One way to use LinkedTube is to take one of your YouTube videos, enter in the information at LinkedTube, and then post that in your blog. Not only will this help increase your views, you can use LinkedTube's button to link to a sales page or you can even use it as a 'Buy Now' button too.

Automation

Since I am pretty lazy, I live by the motto of 'Work smarter, not harder'. Automation encapsulates that idea. The idea of automation is to use services that can do some of the work for you, saving you a lot of time. There are many automation services and software out there, feel free to research more of them. For this book, I focus only on the free services. One such service is a great website called PixelPipe.

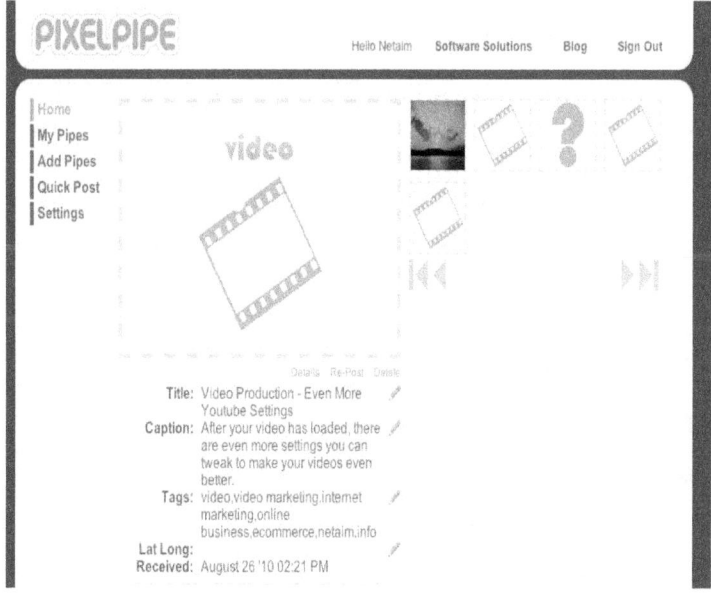

PixelPipe is a free site that can send videos, articles, links, pictures, and more to multiple sites at one time. Once you register (for free), you can search and add 'Pipes' to other websites. 'Pipes' is the site's way of naming different sharing sites such as: Facebook, Blogger, etc. If you click on 'Add Pipes', you can see the list of pipes.

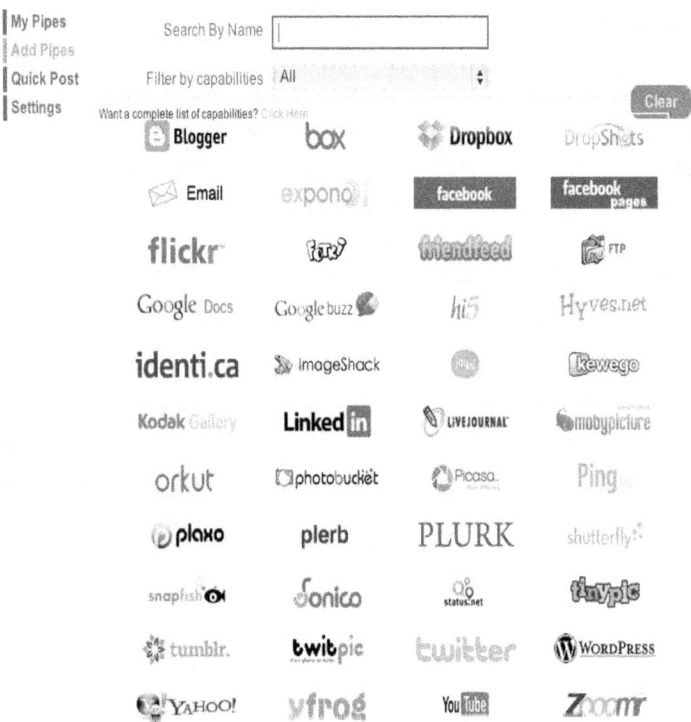

This is a small list of pipes. Be sure to go to PixelPipe.com to see the whole list.

Want a complete list of capabilities? Click Here

You can pick and choose which pipes you want to add. For each pipe that you add to your list, you must have an account. If you see any pipes that you don't have an account for, it's okay, you can sign up for them at any point. In order to make it easier to search for pipes, they have set it up to allow you to search by capability.

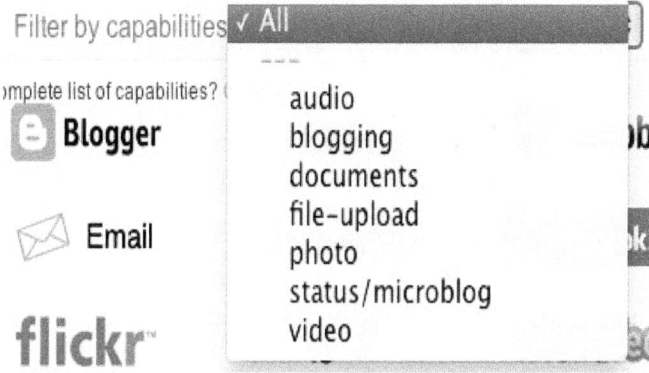

This way, you can pinpoint what pipes you want to focus on. Once you have some pipes set up, you can then send your video out to the world. There are different ways to send your video out. I'm going to cover two different versions while pointing out the pros and cons of both.

1. Send your YouTube link out to your pipes. Sending your YouTube link out to your pipes will help increase your YouTube views. Since this book focuses mainly on YouTube and views, this is the preferred method. However, not all pipes are going to accept YouTube links, so the number of pipes you can send your video out to may be limited. Here's how you would do that:

Click 'Quick Post'

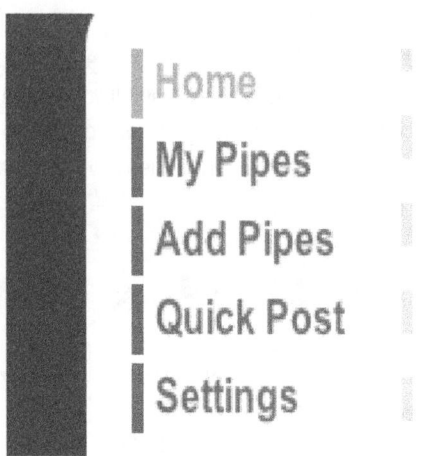

In Quick Post, fill in the required information.

You may have to test out how the body of your post will look on individual pipes; sometimes you may get away with posting the YouTube embed code in the body and it will play fine. Other times, you may have to just post the share link, such as in microblogs or blog posts.

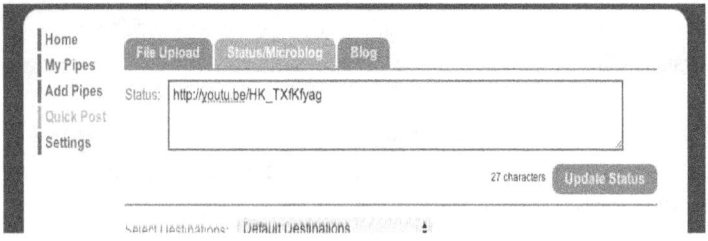

To send your video link to Status/Microblog sites such as Twitter, post the link along with a message - if you desire - in the status box. For most microblog sites, you will only be able to use the YouTube link, as embed codes have too many characters allowed in updates.

http://www.MarcBullard.com

To send your video to blogs, click the 'Blog' tab. Give your video a title and then paste either the embed code or the share link. This is where you may have to do some research to see what works with what pipe. But you only have to do this once.

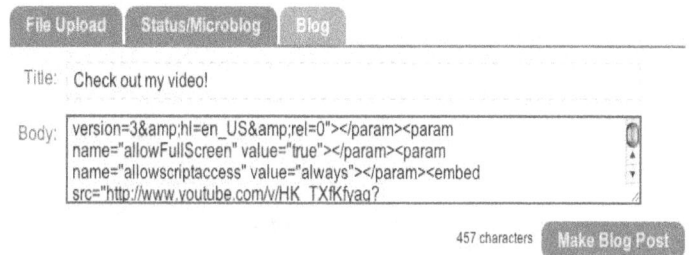

2. Upload your video file to PixelPipe. PixelPipe lets you upload your video file straight from your computer. You can then send that out to your pipes. Going this route will mean your video gets seen but it has nothing to do with YouTube or increasing views. Here's how you do that:

Click on the 'File Upload' tab.

Click the 'Choose File' button and navigate to your video file on your computer. Select the file and begin your upload. Fill in the 'Title', 'Body', and 'Tags' sections. Click the 'Upload' Button.

Just so you know, for each tab - 'File Upload', 'Status/Microblog', 'Blog' - you have the choice of determining exactly what pipes of yours you want to send your post to. PixelPipe shows you a list of the available pipes underneath where you enter information. Each pipe has a check box that you can turn on or off.

Tags: keywords, important keywords, YouTube, anybody readin(

Select Destinations: Default Destinations   ⬍

☑ 🔢 Netaim	☑ ◔ Netaim
☑ audioboo	☑ Netaim
☑ b blipfoto	☑ b box
☑ B brightkite	☑ netaim
☑ Netaim	☑ Netaim
☑ Netaim	☑ dropbox
☑ Netaim	☑ B evernote
☑ netaim	☑ Netaim
☑ eca688fcf6db8bf9	☑ Netaim
☑ marc@antion.com	☑ lifeblob
☑ marc@antion.com	☑ Netaim
☑ Netaim	☑ O orkut
☑ Netaim	☑ picasa

Available 'File Upload' pipes in my account. Yours may be different.

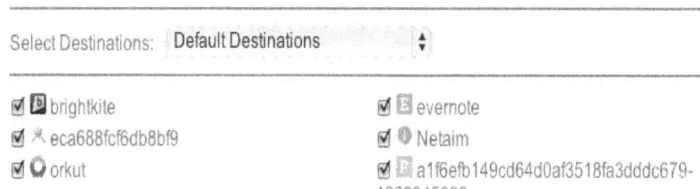

Available 'Status/Microblog' pipes in my account. Yours may be different.

The best solution is to combine both sending your link out and also uploading your file. Uploading your video file will help you upload to other video sharing sites not mentioned in this book. It is an overall good marketing idea to send your video out to video sharing sites other than YouTube. Although YouTube is by far the largest, the other video sharing sites do get enough traffic to not be ignored.

QuietTube - *http://quietube.com/*

Want to watch YouTube videos without all the comments, ads, and extra stuff cluttering up your viewing experience? Try QuietTube, it's free.

quietube: Video without the distractions

To watch web videos without the comments and crap, just drag the button below to your browser's bookmarks bar. On any of the supported video pages, click the bookmark button to watch in peace.

You can then make short URLs too, to send the quietube version to your friends. Easy as.

We support **YouTube**, **BBC iPlayer**, **Viddler**, and **Vimeo**, with more to come...

→ Here's an example.
→ Here's a quick tutorial.

→ Updates on Twitter.

> quietube

↑ Drag this button to your toolbar (Don't click it!)

Or you can use:
→ **Chrome Extension** - with thanks to Chris Burrows
→ **Greasemonkey Script** - with thanks to **Andrew Harrison**

Built by **STML** | Adverts ↓

Broadway Shows
Freecorder Download YouTube Video Free
YouTube to MP3

YouTube "Feather" - *http://www.youtube.com/feather_beta*

The Feather option is perfect for people with slow Internet connections. It limits the features available to the viewer, thereby reducing the total amount of bytes downloaded by your Internet browser. When you turn the feature on,

http://www.MarcBullard.com

201

a small box will appear when you watch videos, alerting you that you are in "Feather" mode. This is still in Beta and may not work with every video.

> You are viewing this on a lightweight version of the video page. Go back to the regular video page?
> Just this once | Permanently

YouTube Channel Gadget - *http://www.google.com/ig/directory?type=gadgets&url=www.google.com/ig/modules/youtube.xml*

The YouTube Channel Gadget is perfect for adding subscribers from outside of YouTube. Simply place the gadget anywhere on your sites and it will provide a featured video as well as a 'Subscribe' button.

YouTube Channel Gadget

By Google

This gadget displays YouTube Videos

15,709 users | ★★★★★ 17 ratings

(Add it now)

✉ Share this gadget

YouTube URL and Embed Tricks

Here are a few neat URL tricks you can use with your videos.

Start your video playing at any time you specify

Let's say you have a video that's 3 minutes long but the good stuff doesn't begin until a minute in. Simply add '**#t=XXmYYs**' (don't use the quotes ') to the share URL. In the example, XX stands for minutes, and YY stands for seconds. So, if I wanted my video to start a minute in, I would add the code '**#t=01m00s**' to the end of the URL.

http://www.MarcBullard.com

View in High Quality

When you provide a link to a video, you have the option to have the link be a high quality version of the video. All you have to do is place a little bit more code at the end of your shared video URL. Simply add '**&fmt=22**' (don't use the quotes ') to the end.

Embed in High Quality

While trick number 1 works for the share link, it won't work with embedded videos. In order to show your embedded video in high quality, simply add '**&ap=%2526fmt%3D22**' (don't use the quotes ').

Autoplay an embedded video

Normally when you embed a video on a site, the player will sit on the site waiting for somebody to hit play. In order to have your video start the instant somebody goes to that page, you simply add the code '**&autoplay=1**' (don't use the quotes ') to the URL. This is also a good way to increase views because every time somebody visits your site, the video starts playing, counting as another view.

Add code here

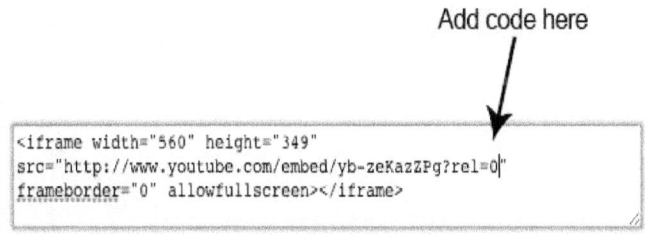

```
<iframe width="560" height="349"
src="http://www.youtube.com/embed/yb-zeKazZPg?rel=0"
frameborder="0" allowfullscreen></iframe>
```

For all of the embed code examples, add the extra code at the end of the video URL. In this case, the URL is http://www.youtube.com/embed/yb-zeKazZPG?rel=0.

Loop an embedded video

If you would like to loop a video so once it finishes, it'll start over again, simply add **'&loop=1'** (don't use quotes ')

Remove the YouTube Logo from the Player with Modest Branding

YouTube now allows the player to contain no YouTube logo, they call this Modest Branding. Take a look at the pictures below.

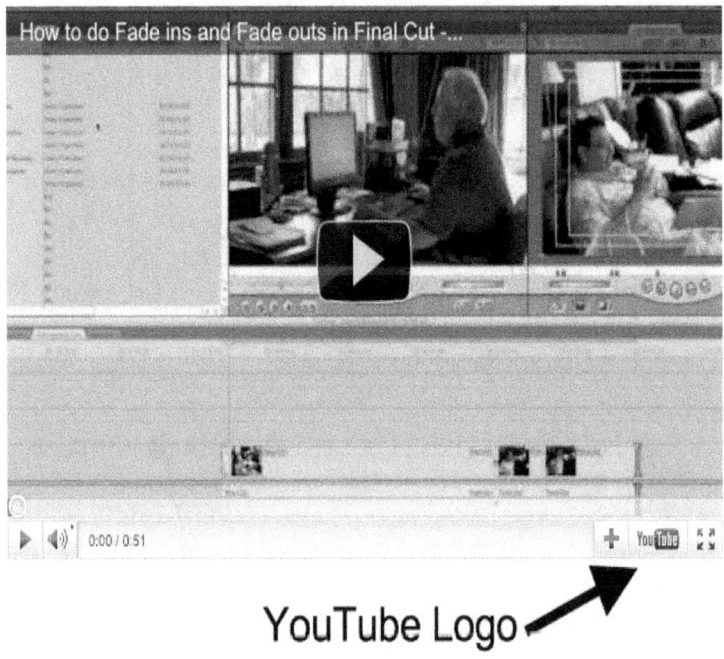

YouTube Logo

When you embed a video on your site, YouTube normally has a small logo in the bottom right of the player. The problem with this is that for some serious businesses, the logo bothers them and so they won't use YouTube for their embedding needs. What YouTube has done is made it easier for businesses to use the YouTube player on their sites by giving them the option to remove the logo.

In order to remove the YouTube logo from the player, all you have to do is insert a small bit of code in the video's embed code. The small bit of code looks like this:

?modestbranding=1

Usually, the embed code looks like this:

<iframe width="560" height="349" src="http://www.youtube.com/embed/7ZNFLFHhPWc?rel=0" frameborder="0" allowfullscreen></iframe>

This embed code will create a player that has the logo. What you need to do is put in the small extra bit of code so it looks like this:

<iframe width="560" height="349" src="http://www.youtube.com/embed/7ZNFLFHhPWc**?modestbranding=1** " frameborder="0" allowfullscreen></iframe>

I put in bold where the code needs to be inserted; your code will not be bolded.

Once you put the extra code in, your video will look like this:

No YouTube Logo

The logo is now removed from the player. The only time you will see the YouTube logo is when a user moves their mouse over the player. The logo then appears in the upper right corner.

Remove Everything from a YouTube Video (Well, almost everything)

Look at the video below:

Other than the deer-in-headlights look I have in this video, what else do you see, or more importantly don't see. There's no player. Also, you can't see it but this video automatically started playing and there's no related videos at the end. If I bring my mouse over the screen, I won't get the same result as the modest branding version. Instead I'll get a small YouTube logo that fades up in the bottom corner and it will fade out when the mouse leaves the screen. Here's how it looks with the mouse hovering over the screen:

Clicking on the screen will pause/play the video. Clicking on the YouTube link will send people to the video on YouTube. This is really cool customization of the YouTube player. Not only would this would be perfect for sales letters, but if you created an unlisted link (page 23), you could embed videos such as video products or webinar replays to only specific people. There's many uses for this.

So do you want to know how to do it? I'm not going to tell you. Just kidding. It is a little complicated so what I'm going to do is provide you with the code already made and you just need to replace one thing. Nice huh?

The code looks like this:

```
<iframe width="560" height="349"
src="http://www.youtube.com/embed/39pjOe5e0m8?rel=0;autoplay=1;contro
ls=0;showinfo=0;modestbranding=1; "frameborder="0"
allowfullscreen></iframe>
```

Now don't let this scare you, there's only one tiny part you need to change and that's the section in bold (**39pjOe5e0m8**). So what you would do is copy this entire code and paste it somewhere safe. Then go to YouTube and find the video you want to embed. Once you find the video, get that video's code. You can find the code in 2 easy places, either at the end of the URL in your browser or in the share link.

 www.youtube.com/watch?v=VzfgcKLMve0&feature=feedrec

Here is your ID in your browser

Link to this video:

http://youtu.be/VzfgcKLMve0

Here is your ID in the share link

Once you have your ID copied, replace the ID I have in **bold** with yours. Then copy and paste the entire code into your blog or website. There you have it, your very own playerless, logoless*, sleek looking video from YouTube.

Many businesses were hesitant to use YouTube because of some of the features they thought they couldn't change. With these features removed now, YouTube is a great decision to use on all of your sites and products. Look at it as free video hosting. Neat, YouTube even can save you money!

Equipment and video tips

Although this section could be a book in itself (hmm.....) I felt I needed to cover at least the basics of equipment and how to set your video up.

Equipment is a subject that gets people nervous, but it need not be. If you break it down, you really only need 4 different components to create quality looking videos.

Camera

The camera is obviously one of the most important factors into creating a very nice looking video. Believe it or not, you don't need an expensive camera. All you need is a compact, hand held camera like a Flip cam. HOWEVER, I highly recommend you **do not** get the Flip video brand. Why? Because they don't contain one extremely important component that you absolutely must have, and that is a microphone input jack. All of the Flip brand video cameras are missing this vital option. Other portable, Flip type cameras do have microphone inputs so make sure the camera you get has one.

So why is a small thing like a microphone jack so important? Well, believe it or not, audio is almost more important than your video. If you have a great shot but your audio is barely there, your video is not worth anything. However, if you have good audio but a bad picture, you can fix your shot in the editing stage. All you'd have to do is cut away to something else, such as your product, and then cut back to the video once your original shot looks good again.

Other features you will want in a camera deal with the quality of the picture. Make sure that whatever one you choose, it is shooting in HD. There are many inexpensive, available cameras that now shoot in 1080. Get one of those.

You will also want to make sure the base of your camera has a threaded area so you can attach it to a tripod. The threaded area will screw right into your tripod, or in other cases, to a plate that will snap into your tripod. Most of these Flip type cameras have this option but don't overlook this.

You don't have to spend a ton of money in order to create a video that looks very good. Start out with the right equipment now and you'll be making videos for a long time.

Find out what camera we recommend and how to shoot with it in order to create Hollywood style videos.

Microphone
Audio is highly important to good videos. If you have bad audio, your video could be unusable. There are three different types of microphones: Handheld, Boom, and Lavalier. Lavalier is the type we are going to use. These mics are the small, newsroom type microphones that clip onto clothing. They come in either wired or wireless. Lavaliers are perfect because they can't be seen and pick up the talent's voice and not much else. Cheap lavalier mics work well for budget conscious marketers.

Lights
Lights can make or break the credibility of a video. Using lights correctly adds to the quality of your production and it doesn't take a lot of money. There are certain lighting techniques that you can use with 3, 2, even 1 light only and your production will still look great. Be sure to learn how to light correctly and your quality production will virtually be complete.

Editing Software
Editing software can be a daunting experience if you don't know what you're doing. I've had the privilege of using at least 10 different editing programs ranging from professional to free and I have found the best bang for your buck. Actually, there are three different programs that are almost identical in features and price. The three programs are:

• Sony Vegas Movie Studio Platinum
• Adobe Premiere Elements

http://www.MarcBullard.com

• Final Cut Express

If you have any of these programs, you are in a good spot to create as many videos as you want. If you are thinking about purchasing one of these programs, they all have their own way of doing things. Once you get one of these editing programs, you will need to get training on how to quickly and easily edit your videos. And believe it or not, there are really only 3 steps you need to take in order to edit your video for the web.

Get the help you need

Learning video may seem like it would have a steep learning curve. But if you have the proper training, including step-by-step instruction, you can quickly learn how to create and market your videos. The list below provides very basic information on creating videos.

Scripting

When it comes to online video for marketing, there are two specific categories of video you should be familiar with. The two types of videos you're going to be producing are:

1. Videos that welcome people to your website

2. Videos that market and drive traffic to your website.

They are two totally different styles, not necessarily in the way they look or any of the framing or lighting or things that I'm going to talk about.
You always want them to be as nice as they possibly can on each one of those. But you just want to keep in mind that you are trying to drive traffic so you want to say different kinds of things.

The scripting is very important in terms of getting people to a website where you want to talk about benefits and the things that you have, maybe freebies that people can pick up. Usually, there is going to be an opt-in box on your website, and this is how you're going to use your videos to capture leads and build an email list.

These videos are the tool you're using to sell yourself just like a presentation, and you're going to be leading people to a conversion. A conversion could be a thing, a sign up, or a purchase. Just going to the website itself is a conversion. But videos are meant to convert so these marketing videos are made specifically to tell as much as you can without giving away everything. All of the important information is on the website.

For instance say, 'if you want to learn the secret to great leadership for teenagers so they can build a life for themselves, I have all the information over on my website.' You want to make sure that you're leading people there and not giving away too much. People will have no reason to visit the website if you've given too much information.

So it's a matter of carefully scripting, carefully leading them to the website. Now, the video that welcomes people is for introducing yourself. If someone is at the website, you get to explain what's around the website, help them navigate around by even pointing to different parts of the website like 'sign up in the box on the right-hand corner'. You may even want to reference that with your fingers or navigate around, click the different tabs to lead them around the site. So it's a virtual, visual lead around the site instead of letting them just struggle on their own.

Creating scripts for each type of video is a great idea. Once you have a basic script, all you have to do is replace the keywords in that script over and over again, creating a lot of videos quickly.

* Bonus Script Point

http://www.MarcBullard.com

Many people fear they will forget what they're going to say in their video. One expensive option to consider is a teleprompter. A teleprompter projects your lines onto a screen that you can read off of. Most news stations use teleprompters. The poor man's version of a teleprompter is to take your script, print it out with large font on paper, and then tape that paper to the bottom of your camera, just out of view of the lens. Now you can read your script while the shot looks like you're simply looking at the camera.

Shooting Tips
When it comes to shooting your video, there are a few things you should take into account in order to have a great looking video.

• No striped shirts or blouses or tight patterns
Striped shirts or blouses with tight, intricate patterns can cause the camera to do some weird things. Most importantly, patterns can cause a 'shimmering' effect to the camera. This shimmering can be distracting, taking away from the viewer getting the most out of your content.

• No dangle jewelry
Jewelry that dangles can be an audio nightmare. Not only can it create an annoying jingle every time it's wiggled, it can also bump the mic. This bump can go unnoticed while shooting but can be a pain to deal with once you get to the editing stage.

• Color Choice
The color choice of your shirt can make or break your video. Strong red colors can have a harsh effect on the camera, causing the red to bleed. Depending on the background, black shirts can also be a bad idea. Good colors to consider are nice, neutral tones such as any pastel colors, light blue, grey, tan, and even brown.

• Wait a few seconds before speaking to give room at the beginning for a fade in

http://www.MarcBullard.com

This tip will save you a lot of time when it comes to editing. At the beginning of your video, you may want to fade in. That is, dissolve from a black screen into the shot. When you start recording, give the camera a few seconds of recording before you start speaking. You should also do the same thing at the end of your video.

• Smile at the end
At the end of your video, be sure to smile and look right at the camera. This is a welcoming way to end your video and it gives your editor time to fade out, or to throw some graphics up on the screen.

•Use bullet points, not a whole script
Earlier, we gave you a bonus tip about the poor man's teleprompter. Although this is still a good idea, it's not a good idea to write out your entire script. We've found that videos which don't have a whole script to be the best and most natural sounding video. If you really need something to help you, put bullet points on your teleprompter instead.

• Say your website without the "WWW"
Saying the name of your website on your video is a good idea. However, it can be a major tongue twister having to say the 'www' part. Leave that part out. These days, everybody knows that websites begin with 'www'.

Sticky Sites
How long someone stays on a website is one of the determining factors of search positioning. Google likes to know that people are staying on a website. The average is six seconds for someone to visit a website and then leave but if they're on there for 30 seconds or more the search engines realize that people are staying there because this site must be good and it must have information that is critical to them. I call that stickiness.

You want your site to be sticky. Stickiness is also good for your Youtube channel. Two ways to make your channel sticky are: 1. Create engaging videos that keep your viewer watching for as long as you can keep them, and 2. Put as many videos on your channel as you can, giving your viewers more options.

Design of Video

Backgrounds

Backgrounds are important. The most important factor I'm talking about here is complementary backgrounds. The background conveys an unconscious visual stimuli in the viewers so they know that you're the expert on something. For instance, if you are a lawyer, you should be sitting at a desk with some books behind you that make you look knowledgeable, not in a funeral parlor or something that doesn't have anything to do with a lawyer.

If you do have a distracting background, such as a funeral parlor, people get distracted and start asking themselves, "Why is he at a funeral parlor? I wonder why he's at a funeral parlor?" Meanwhile they're missing a lot of important content.

Closing Credits

This book could easily double in size if I were to go into detail about the actual production process of making your videos. Hopefully, you either know what you are doing when it comes to creating videos or you have some sort of help in doing so. If you are neither inclined in video production or in contact with somebody who is, don't despair, there is help out there. One great place to get help is to contact me, the author of this book, Marc Bullard. You can email me at bullard.marc@gmail.com or feel free to check out my website MarcBullard.com to discover everything I can do for you.

Also, for more information on video production, video marketing, or online marketing in general feel free to check out these sites. I am an active contributor to all of them:

MarcBullard.com
TopInternetExperts.com
TopInternetConsulting.com
Netaim.info
YouTube Channel - infomarketingexperts
Twitter - TopNetExperts

Hopefully, with the information in this book, you will be well on your way to gaining customers through the ever-growing world of YouTube. Best of luck!

About the Author

Marc Bullard has over 14 years of combined experience with video production, online businesses, and video marketing. He has a Bachelor's degree in Video Production from Stevenson University and a Master's in Education with Technology from Ashford University. Currently, he is the 'video guy' for Internet marketing guru Tom Antion. Marc also runs a marketing blog with online marketing expert and business partner Colin Martin. Marc and Colin also own Netaim.info, the world's largest Internet marketing database, containing over 600 articles and over 200 audio/video recordings covering everything on Internet marketing; including the Millionaire Marketer's Club, a club that offers 2 live calls a month with Colin and Marc for only $9.95/month. He also offers consulting and virtual assistance services as well.

In his spare time Marc likes to be at the beach, especially surfing, or hanging out with his wife Kara and new baby son Nateo.

http://www.MarcBullard.com

Notes

www.ingramcontent.com/pod-product-compliance
Lightning Source LLC
Chambersburg PA
CBHW051454170526
45166CB00001B/244